THE VALIANT BOOK

MARQUE
PUBLISHING COMPANY

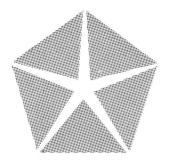

THE VALIANT BOOK

A history of Chrysler Australia's Valiant
1962-1981

by Tony Davis

THE VALIANT BOOK was written by TONY DAVIS and first published in 1987 by MARQUE PUBLISHING COMPANY, PO Box 203, Hurstville, NSW 2220.

© Copyright 1987 Marque Publishing Company.

The Valiant Book
ISBN 0 947079 00 9

Proudly produced wholly within Australia.

Set by Terry Clark Typesetting (Kogarah, NSW).
Design and layout by Tony Davis/Cover by Irene Meier.
Printed by Robert Burton Printers (Sefton, NSW).
Distributed by Kirby Book Company Pty Limited,
Private Bag No. 19, P.O. Alexandria NSW 2015

The author and publishers are grateful to those who provided assistance, most notably Phil Gander, Ewan Kennedy, Anne Sahlin, John Wright and the staff of Mitsubishi Motors Australia Limited.

Special thanks are offered to Barry Lake (editor of *Modern Motor*), Peter Robinson (editor of *Wheels*) and Max Stahl (editor of *Racing Car News*) for permission to reproduce original magazine reports.

INTRODUCTION

This is the first complete model history of Australian-made Valiants ever published.

By giving all relevant specifications and details of each model, plus photos, original road tests, reproductions of historic sales brochures and additional information on the history of the Chrysler Australia (later Mitsubishi Motors Australia) company, this book provides a valuable and interesting reference guide for owners and enthusiasts alike.

It forms an important part of the plans of the MARQUE PUBLISHING COMPANY to document Australian motoring history.

The author, Tony Davis, is a former newspaper reporter whose lifelong interest in cars led him into full-time motoring journalism.

He has written for newspapers and magazines, was General Editor of the acclaimed *Macquarie Dictionary of Motoring* and is currently working on several other motoring books.

LIST OF CONTENTS

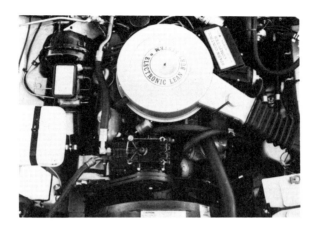

SPECIAL NOTE ON METRIC MOTORING AND POWER OUTPUT

The question of metric and imperial measures gave us hell. The figures given in the early road tests are in imperial measures and, to allow comparisons, it became necessary to give some other figures in similar units.

Furthermore, many Valiant engines were named after their capacity in cubic inches. They are still referred to as the 215, 245, 360 etc.

To clarify things, we have given both metric and imperial measures where necessary.

Power output figures are particularly confusing. Not only are there different units in which power can be measured, but a variety of systems is used to arrive at these units.

We have published the power output figures released by Chrysler at the time of each model's release. However, at various times in Australian motoring history, different methods of measuring power have been in vogue. These methods will produce different output figures from the same engine, so an accurate power output comparison between cars of different eras is not possible.

In the early days of motoring, the lack of an agreed method for measuring power led to the widespread use of an artificial system. Called RAC Horsepower or Taxable Horsepower, it was derived from a formula which included the bore diameter and the number of cylinders. It was expressed in rated horsepower (HP).

Between the World Wars there was a shift towards the use of brake horsepower (bhp). This is the power developed by an engine when spinning at a given speed, as measured by a dynamometer.

The US system of measuring brake horsepower, called SAE, became popular in Australia from the 1940s. An SAE figure (derived from test procedures developed by the Society of Automotive Engineers) provided the gross power output of an engine without the exhaust system and some ancillary equipment fitted. It was favoured by some companies because it flattered the engine, allowing the company to come up with very impressive output figures during horsepower 'wars'.

Rated horsepower still appeared from time to time during the 1960s and 1970s. When Chrysler Australia released the first Valiant, they described it as a 27.7 HP car while claiming 145 bhp.

In the early 1970s there was an industry trend in Australia towards net horsepower. This was measured with most, or all, engine equipment attached and provided a lower but more realistic indication of usable output.

Nevertheless, there were still different test procedures for arriving at the net figures.

Since 1976, when Australia changed to the SI Metric system, power has usually been given in net kilowatts, with 75 kW being approximately equal to 100 bhp. The system for measuring this 'installed power' is based on an Australian standard similar to the German DIN system.

We have converted all figures (except rated horsepower) to kilowatts, and as a general rule, you can assume figures are 'gross' up to the mid 1970s and then 'net' until the 1980s when 'installed' figures became almost universal.

INTRODUCING THE VALIANT

The Chrysler name and the world-famous Pentastar symbol have not been used in Australia since 1981. But for more than 50 years Australians bought new Chrysler cars for every job from towing the family boat to racing around circuits and charging across the continent.

Of the many brands sold by Chrysler Australia Ltd, one name stands out — Valiant.

More than half-a-million Valiants were built and sold down-under between 1962 and 1981 and a large proportion are still giving loyal service.

Chrysler Australia Ltd was a subsidiary of the US Chrysler Corporation, a giant multinational concern started by the remarkable Walter P. Chrysler.

Walter P. Chrysler, a former railway worker, made his reputation working for Buick, then took over the former Maxwell Motor Company which was heavily in debt. Soon afterwards he bought the Chalmers company and, in 1924, launched a completely new car called Chrysler. This six-cylinder model had a number of engineering refinements including four-wheel hydraulic brakes.

Chrysler cars came to Australia during the 1920s and, in 1935, 18 independent agents formed Chrysler-Dodge-De Soto Distributors (Australia) Pty Ltd. The distributors used their combined strength to purchase and market Plymouth, Dodge and De Soto vehicles. The company acquired a controlling interest in T.J. Richards & Sons, a highly successful Adelaide-based body-building company which had been the main competitor for Holden's body builders since 1922.

For several years T.J. Richards had designed and fitted bodies to locally made Chrysler vehicles. For the 1937-38 selling season, T.J. Richards beat Holden's to the punch by producing Australia's first all-steel sedan body.

During WW2 Chrysler-Dodge-De Soto Distributors manufactured munitions and aircraft components. Most of the skilled workforce remained when the firm returned to motor vehicle production in 1945. The company was entirely owned by Australians

ABOVE: The 1957 Chrysler Royal.
PREVIOUS PAGE: Walter Chrysler and an early Chrysler car.

until June 1951 when Chrysler Corporation bought a controlling interest and changed the name to Chrysler Australia Ltd.

A vigorous expansion plan followed, and inspired by the success of Holden, Chrysler Australia aimed at producing a range of cars and light commercial vehicles with 90 per cent local content. While this plan was being implemented, the company continued assembling and partly manufacturing a range of six-cylinder and eight-cylinder Royal and Dodge Phoenix vehicles, based on US designs.

Towards the end of 1958 Chrysler Corporation acquired a 30 per cent interest in Simca Automobiles of France, thus enabling Chrysler Australia to import and assemble a range of Simca cars.

Chrysler Australia is best known, however, for the Valiant, which was introduced in January 1962. The Valiant was a sensation — and it arrived at just the right time.

In the very early 1960s Chrysler's operation had been looking shaky with its range of big American cars continually losing ground to the all-conquering Holden. Simca sales had tapered off, and with the release of the Ford Falcon, Chrysler's problems became worse.

The response came in early 1961 when company officials devised a plan to assemble a US-designed compact six-cylinder car in Australia. To get the new model released as soon as possible, the firm imported just over 1000 US-built R Series Valiant sedans. These were assembled in the Mile End plant at Adelaide, and when they hit the showroom floors in early 1962, the response left no doubt that Australians were going to fall for the new brand in a big way.

By the time the R Series went on sale (it sold out within days!), Chrysler had imported a large number of updated S Series sedans and local assembly had already begun. Chrysler assembled 10 000 Valiants in 1962 — lifting its registration figures for the year by 146 per cent. But the company still could not meet the demand.

The Simca Aronde on the racetrack and (BELOW) in an 'Australiana' publicity shot.

This spectacular introduction was the start of a 20-year story which saw Valiant's fortunes snowball for a while and then slide in dramatic fashion.

The 1962 Valiant was slightly dearer than the equivalent Holden and Falcon models but it was bigger and far more powerful. It immediately won a reputation for being a superior performer and its popularity led Chrysler into a $36 million expansion plan to build 50 000 units a year, with local content increasing progressively.

Construction of the Tonsley Park manufacturing plant began in 1963, and by May of that year, the 'Australian Valiant' sedan was introduced. With high local content and a design adapted for local conditions, this 'AP5' Valiant strengthened the brand's position. The Australian Valiant AP5 station wagon followed in November 1963.

In March 1964 the first Valiant was completed at the new plant, and in April it was announced that the $36 million expansion program had been doubled to $72 million.

In 1965 Chrysler took over Rootes Australia and acquired that company's Melbourne manufacturing and assembling facilities. In 1967 Chrysler's Lonsdale engine plant opened and the company gained third place in the national sales chart, with 13.5 per cent of the new vehicle market.

Local content kept rising in leaps and bounds. It went from 1962's minor assembly work on the R and S Series to 65 per cent in 1965 and an average of 95 per cent in 1967. By that year some models had as much as 97 per cent local content.

The mid-to-late 1960s were halcyon times for Chrysler because the company could not satisfy demand despite regular increases in production. By this time, Chrysler was the eleventh largest company (of any kind) in Australia and the second largest exporter of cars. 1969 was Chrysler's best year with 42 654 Valiants sold. Net profit was a record $7 225 931 and total Chrysler Australia Ltd sales stood at 66 948 units.

Most people in 1969 thought that Chrysler's great automotive success would continue into the 1970s, but it was not to be. A series of misfortunes, fuel crises, quality control problems, unpopular models and blunders saw the Valiant lose sales during the early 1970s. The marque then slipped further and further down the list of best-sellers, despite such trump cards as the mighty Charger sports coupe.

Many problems were sorted out and the

The 1960 Chrysler Royal introduced dual headlights and triple tail-lights but was still no match for Holden.

company became the local pioneer of such features as electronic ignition and computer-aided fuel management. It also produced the fastest-accelerating Australian production car ever made.

But the fightback came too late — public confidence was down, and with reduced sales and an ailing US parent company, the funds needed to retool for new models were no longer available.

In retrospect it seems one major mistake was that Valiant prices were held back in the late 1960s to meet the Holden and Ford head-on. When this happened, people seemed to stop considering the car to be 'a cut above' its opposition.

By 1977 Valiant was still producing a variation of its six-year-old VH model. Sales that year slumped to 17 500 units. Nevertheless, the company was making good progress in the smaller-car field. The US parent company had bought into the vehicle division of the Japanese Mitsubishi company and in 1971 Chrysler Australia arranged to assemble and distribute Mitsubishi's Galant.

The Galant wore a Valiant badge and succeeded brilliantly in Australia, giving Chrysler the share of the small-car market it had failed to win with the Simca and Hillman. Chrysler expanded once again, this time to manufacture the Sigma, a local version of Mitsubishi's Japanese Galant model. The factory continued producing Valiants in ever diminishing numbers but with higher standards of equipment and finish.

1962 R Series Valiant.

1974 VJ Valiant Charger.

Small-car sales went from strength to strength and in 1978 Sigma became the top-selling four-cylinder vehicle on the market. Despite this success, Chrysler Australia Ltd ran into severe financial problems. In the US the Chrysler Corporation had run into even harder times and was on the brink of being closed.

Former Ford president Lee Iacocca took charge of the US Chrysler Corporation during the late 1970s and set in motion some drastic measures to keep the company afloat. These included selling off almost all of Chrysler's overseas interests, including the Australian operation.

Ninety-nine per cent of the equity of Chrysler Australia Ltd was acquired by Mitsubishi, and in October 1980 the name was changed to Mitsubishi Motors Australia Ltd.

In all the years Chrysler Australia had operated, not a single dollar had been sent back to the parent company. All returns had been ploughed back into the local company — a fact which made all employees rightfully proud.

By the mid-1980s Iacocca had the US Chrysler Corporation firmly on its feet and making record profits (the story was later told in *Iacocca — An Autobiography*, one of the best selling books of all time). But the success in the US came too late for the Australian subsidiary. Mitsubishi continued to make Valiants (with Chrysler badges) for a short while — but the end was in sight.

The last Valiant was produced in August 1981. By that time 13 model series had been released with a total of 565 338 units built.

During 1962 the original R Series Valiant had been replaced by the S Series. This was followed by the AP5 (1963), AP6 (1965), VC (1966), VE (1967), VF (1969), VG (1970), VH (1971), VJ (1973), VK (1975), CL (1976), and CM (1978).

Of these the VJ was the biggest seller, with 90 865 units built. The least successful model was the final design, the CM, selling only 16 005 units in three years.

The story of each Valiant model — from the first US-sourced 'R' to the last dinki-di 'CM' — follows.

R SERIES (1962)

The gunmetal dash.

There was a time when General Motors-Holden's was virtually unchallenged. For more than ten years a succession of Holden models ruled the roost.

In September 1960 Ford's XK Falcon arrived and was widely judged to be better looking than the FB Holden. Furthermore, it was built by a company determined to cut a big hole in The General's lucrative market.

For GM-H that was shock number one. January 1962 brought shock number two — a brand-new car which immediately won over the public with its combination of power, styling and luxury.

This car was made by Chrysler and its name was Valiant.

'The Big Three' — the trinity which would spend the 1960s and 1970s fighting tooth and nail for the affections and money of the Australian car buyer — was born.

In a press release marked 'Not for Publication before 11 am January 18, 1962', Chrysler announced:

'VALIANT SUITED TO AUSTRALIA — Engineers road-tested the Valiant over thousands of miles to ensure it was entirely suited to Australian conditions.

The Valiant passed all tests with flying colors. Figures obtained with Australian fuels:
— Top speed, one way, 94 mph.
— Acceleration, standing quarter-mile, 19.5 sec.
— Economy proved exceptional for a 27.7 HP [rated] six-cylinder car.

One modification made to the Valiant . . . was the fitting of 14 inch wheels to give increased ground clearance.'

With this release, Australia was introduced to the Valiant at a price of 1299 pounds ($2598) including tax for the three-speed standard model with floor-mounted gearlever. A state-of-the-art, three-speed, push-button automatic transmission was available for an extra 136 pounds ($272).

The Valiant which appeared on showroom

floors in January 1962 was locally assembled from US parts. Called the R Series (or RV-1), it was based on an American car sold in various countries at that time wearing a Dodge or a Plymouth badge.

Local planning had started in early 1961 when Chrysler Australia imported a sample car with a 2.8-litre (170 cubic inches) engine and three-speed manual transmission. This car had excellent performance and very good economy, but Chrysler wanted a marketing edge. As a result, local officials decided to fit the Valiant with the bigger of the two engines offered with the car in the US. This was a 3.69-litre (225 cubic inches), overhead-valve, six-cylinder engine inclined at 30 degrees to the right.

This 'Slant Six' engine produced 109 kW (145 bhp) and 291 Nm (215 lb/ft) of torque. Locals who tested the car quickly found that although Chrysler claimed 94 mph (150 km/h) top speed and a 19.5 second quarter mile, the new car could almost touch 100 mph (161 km/h) and run the standing quarter mile in about 18.8 seconds. That made it far quicker than the 1962 Holden or Falcon.

The then-current EK Holden was still running on the 'Grey' motor, virtually unchanged since 1948. It developed just 56 kW (75 bhp), little more than half that of the Valiant. The standard XK Falcon engine was a bit better —

developing 67.5 kW (90 bhp) — but the car already had a bad name for durability. There was no questioning the strength of the large and solid Valiant.

Chrysler's new entry had a dynamic effect on the local public and on the motoring press, which went so far as to describe its low-slung body styling as 'space age'. They praised its lively performance, manoeuvrability, standard of finish, handling, quality of ride and stopping power.

There were reservations about some things: the non-synchromesh first gear, the 12.3 L/100 km (23 mpg) fuel consumption, the small 48-litre (10 gallons) fuel tank, the lack of a heater and the fake spare tyre mount on the rear boot lid (dubbed the 'garbage-bin lid' by some). Some writers described the sculptured, curved look as 'a panel beater's nightmare' but all in all they found the Valiant to be 'fundamentally good' and a 'pleasure to drive'.

Seats were of the bench type and instrumentation was pretty basic, with a speedo next to a matching dial containing minor gauges. The dials were set on a 'gunmetal' aluminium panel — an idea which didn't catch on with other Australian makers until the early 1970s. With the R Series, Chrysler became the first of the Big Three to use an alternator instead of the then-usual generator (an alternator is smaller and lighter and delivers alternating

The 'space age' profile.

current without the need for a separate rectifier).

The most pleasing things about the Valiant were its looks, size and power. It was no surprise that the first batch of 1008 'R' models sold out within days of appearing on the showroom floors.

Within weeks Chrysler put on sale a batch of the later US model — the 'S' type — and the company was assembling these as quickly as possible. By year's end around 10 000 Valiants had been sold!

RIGHT and BELOW: Early 'R' publicity shots.

wheels

AUSTRALIA'S TOP MOTORING MAGAZINE

2'6

MARCH, 1962

Registered at the G.P.O., Sydney, for
transmission by post as a periodical.

SPECIAL REPORT: 1962 SPORTS CARS

Here, at last is the long-awaited Valiant. It is a true compact car and its height is surprisingly low. It has been Australianised.

VALIANT --

CHRYSLER'S PUNCH-FOR-PRICE CAR

Loaded with power, but costing a mere £1299 with stick shift, the Valiant is one of Australia's top performing cars on a £ for £ basis.

FOR the last 30 years, the vast majority of car buyers in America have bought their motor cars from what is known as the Big Three.

They were — and are — General Motors, Ford and Chrysler, in that order on sales volume.

The same was generally the case in Australia, too, in the decade before the Second World War and even until severe dollar restrictions were introduced about 14 years ago.

But only two of the Big Three — General Motors and Ford — have seemed to fight hard, especially in the last couple of years, to retain a grip on their large segments of our car market.

They have done this mainly by increasing their manufacturing capacity in Australia and — in 1948 in GM's case, and 1960 as far as Ford were concerned — by producing all-Australian-made cars.

The third of the Big Three has, on the other, slipped as far as percentage of the car market is concerned. It's first really big mistake (you can call it that, by being wise after the event) was the decision early in the 1950's to concentrate on local production of existing BIG American Chrysler models. The Plymouths, Dodges and DeSotos that had been in such demand in earlier decades, proved to have declining interest to a market already well geared to the Holden and all it offered in the way of competitive in-

itial price, low running costs and sensible size. On a dwindling big car market, Chrysler Australia found itself stuck with the outdated Royal range.

It kept itself alive only by declining to make expensive major changes to the Royal, by selling Simcas and by going into business as one of Australia's largest tool and die makers.

But now, Chrysler looks set for a change in fortune. The long-awaited release in Australia of the American compact Valiant, at a surprisingly competitive price, is clearly a big initial move in a Chrysler campaign to take, slowly perhaps, an increasing share of the Australian market.

At £1299, including sales tax, the standard model Valiant is £130 dearer than the equivalent Holden (the Special) and £100 above the equivalent Falcon (the deluxe).

The optional automatic transmission will add £136 to the Valiant's price, making that transmission about £17 to £18 dearer than the

Manual model has a gear change on the floor, offset in favor of the driver. Automatic is optional for £136 more.

competitive automatics from GMH and Ford.

Does it offer that much more? A rushed test done specially for WHEELS within minutes of the Valiant's release would indicate that it certainly does offer more motor car and more genuine driving fun than the cars Chrysler is boldly pitting the Valiant against.

An unusual design, the Valiant stands out as a highly distinctive and individual motor car. Identical in appearance to the current American model it is being assembled from largely imported parts on a much smaller volume than Holden and Falcon are being completely made in Australia.

The test car was full of improvements over its American - built cousins.

It was, for a start, an immeasurably better quality car, as far as finish is concerned, than the American Valiant. Body welds were clean and strong, all the doors shut easily with a nice click, body panels were smooth and fitted correctly and the paintwork was first class — indeed the best I have yet seen from Chrysler Australia. This is all praise that could not be made of the American job.

That the local Valiant has been put together with great thought for Australian conditions is clear from the specifications

The engine is the most powerful six that could be fitted to the Valiant

The 145 bhp engine lies slightly to one side, but this gives good access to most parts, reduces bonnet height

from the variety made by the parent company. Indeed, in America, this 220 cu in slanted motor is not offered in the Valiant at all. It is primarily a Plymouth engine.

Inclined to the right at 30 degrees,

the overhead valve engine develops 145 brake horsepower — enough to give it vivid acceleration, a high top speed and all the strength needed for average Australian conditions, and a lot of abnormal conditions as well.

Luggage boot is large, but filler pipe pokes in too far for comfort.

The only complaint back seat travellers are likely to have is an understandable lack of leg and knee room when the front seat is pushed right back. All doors of the Valiant are fitted with armrests, another fairly rare feature. The windows in all the doors, retract fully into them, when in the open position — a commendable feature in hot Australia.

This car is going to appeal to a lot of people who like their motor cars to behave properly on the road. The suspension — independent torsion bars at the front and long, wide semi-elliptics at the back — gives the Valiant a firm but quite comfortable ride.

On bad cobblestones, I experienced a fair amount of front end shake at speed, but the Valiant held true to its course and little of the vibration came through the recirculating ball steering system.

On the open road, however, the Valiant handled extremely well. There was no nose dive under braking and practically no body roll at all on fast corners. The Valiant sat truly at all times and cornered with almost neutral steering characteristics. Only under extreme conditions, did a very slight understeer show itself.

Very fast cruising would be a great delight in this car — it sits down well on the road, mechanical noise is barely a murmur and there is no wind noise at all, unless you open the quarter vent windows, and even then the wind is hardly noticeable.

There are points on which the Valiant can be criticised, notably an over-large turning circle, but generally it is a worthy entrant by Chrysler in the Australian mass market stakes.   #

Accessibility to most service parts under the bonnet is exceptionally good. There is a ton of room around this big powerful motor and the only parts that seemed at all hard to get at were the spark plugs.

It was an even greater annoyance, then, than it might otherwise have been to find that the Valiant had no internal bonnet lock.

An interesting feature of the engine compartment was the fitting of a Chrysler alternator instead of the conventional generator. Chrysler, which also fits this type of unit to the Australian-assembled Dodge, claims it is more powerful and reliable than the generator. Be that as it may, the alternator certainly takes up less space under the bonnet.

To my mind one of the outstanding features of the Valiant was the very sensible and comfortable driving position.

The seat was firm and had a broad adjustment, enhanced by a slight tilt as the seat was moved back to the position of maximum driver leg room.

The instruments were neatly clustered in a binnacle directly in front of the driver and easily seen through the top half of the steering wheel.

They consisted of a big circular speedo somewhat unnecessarily calibrated to 110 mph and a cluster of instruments in a dial as big as the speedo containing a fuel gauge, ammeter, temperature gauge and oil warning light.

Trafficator switch was on the left of the steering column within fingertip reach of the rim, while the handbrake was under the dash on the right of the column.

The handbrake seemed flimsy on first acquaintance, but it proved easy to operate and had a strong action.

Foot pedals were well placed, but gave rise to two small grumbles. The accelerator organ-type pedal had a very strong return spring and could become very tiring on a speedy long trip. The dipper switch was poorly placed half under the right edge of the clutch pedal. I found my left foot constantly fouling it and unless my foot was exactly square in the middle of the clutch pedal, I could not get the pedal to go right to the floor. In the hands of lackadaisical owners, the Valiant could well give clutch and gear trouble, thanks to this poor placement.

Vision was exceptionally good in all directions, except out the left hand side of the windscreen where distortion, on the test car at any rate, was as bad as I have ever seen.

The transmission tunnel was not excessively high and there would be little difficulty fitting in six people. The same floor plan is used for the automatic model, so this, too, can be classed as a six seater.

Chrysler has shown great ingenuity with the gear change arrangements on the standard model. The lever comes out of the floor, well to the right of the transmission tunnel and curls like a charmed cobra around the edge of the seat to bring the lever knob very close indeed to the driver's left thigh.

The knob could not be better placed from the driver's point of view — and it allows the third passenger in the front to be unhampered by cog swapping.

The change itself is quite good, although it suffers from a certain mushiness thanks to the length and curl of the lever. Unfortunately there is no synchromesh on first gear, and the movement from first to second is a bit on the long side.

Back seat passengers are better catered for than in most cars of this class. The back seat is nicely raked and well padded. Getting in and out of the car is quite easy and head room is better than in many quite big cars.

The Valiant features some rather elaborate body pressings which include fake spare wheel on boot lid and tail lamps.

wheels ROAD TEST

TECHNICAL DETAILS
OF THE
CHRYSLER VALIANT.

PERFORMANCE

TOP SPEED:

Average	96.8 mph
Best one-way run	98.9 mph

MAXIMUM SPEED IN GEARS:

First	42 mph
Second	70 mph

ACCELERATION:

Standing Quarter Mile:

Fastest run	19.3 sec
Average of all runs	19.4 sec
0 to 30 mph	4.0 sec
0 to 40 mph	4.3 sec
0 to 50 mph	9.45 sec
0 to 60 mph	**11.5 sec**
0 to 70 mph	18.9 sec
0 to 80 mph	23.7 sec
20 to 40 mph	6.65 sec
30 to 50 mph	6.9 sec
40 to 60 mph	5.25 sec

GO-TO-WHOA:

0-60-0 mph	18.5 sec

SPEEDO ERROR:

Indicated	Actual
30 mph	31.1 mph
50 mph	50.2 mph
70 mph	68.9 mph

FUEL CONSUMPTION:

21 mpg — mainly city driving.

PRICE:

£1299.

TEST CAR FROM:

Chrysler Australia Ltd.

SPECIFICATIONS

ENGINE:

Cylinders	Six, in-line, inclined 30 deg. to right
Bore and Stroke	3.4 x 4.125 in
Cubic capacity	3688 cc
Compression ratio	8.2 to 1
Carburettor	Single downdraught
Power at rpm	145 at 4000
Maximum torque	215 lb/ft at 2800 rpm

TRANSMISSION:

Type	Three-speed manual

Ratios:

First	**2.71**
Second	**1.83**
Top	**1.00**
Reverse	**3.49**

SUSPENSION:

Front	Independent, torsion bars
Rear	Semi-eliptic leaf springs
Shockers	Telescopic, double action

STEERING:

Type	Re-circulating ball
Turns L. to L.	**4½**
Circle	**40 ft**

BRAKES:

Type	Drum and shoes

DIMENSIONS:

Wheelbase	8 ft 10½ ins
Track front	4 ft 8 in
Track rear	4 ft 7½ in
Length	15 ft 3 7/10 in
Width	5 ft 10.4 in
Height	4 ft 7 in

TYRES:

Size	5.90 by 14

WEIGHT:

Kerb	23¼ cwt

The Valiant 'R' wagon which never made it downunder.

S SERIES (1962)

The S series had everything that made the R series successful. Promotion was heavy — Chrysler could at last supply in volume.

The S Series (or SV-1) Valiant was a minor refinement of the R Series, but it enhanced the Valiant's image of being 'a cut above average'.

Like its predecessor, the S Series was a locally assembled US design and was offered to the Australian public in only one form — four-door sedan.

The relatively low number of the earlier R Series Valiants (1008) had been imported to get the car established as quickly as possible. The enthusiasm with which the Australian public received them had caused an earlier clearance than expected but, luckily, local production of the S was already well under way.

Chrysler's managing director, David H. Brown, boasted that many improvements had been embodied in the S Series Valiant. These included a steering column gearshift (replacing the floor lever), greater braking area, new grille design, cleaner boot line

(omitting the fake wheel moulding), a larger 53-litre (11.7 gallons) fuel tank and a corrosion resistant exhaust muffler.

New round tail-lights were fitted below the rear fins which had housed the lights on the R Series Valiant.

A sealed chassis system made lubrication at 3200 km (2000 miles) intervals no longer necessary — Chrysler said that 51 200 km (32 000 miles) intervals were sufficient for everything but the front end, which still required regular greasing.

With the new model the price went up 16 pounds to 1255 pounds ($2510) for the standard model and 1385 pounds ($2670) for the automatic. But few buyers, if any, were deterred. There was still a waiting period of several months.

10 009 S Series Valiants were made before Chrysler offered a completely new body with the 'Aussie Valiant', the AP5.

VALIANT

by CHRYSLER...the finest of the '3'

1. YOU BENEFIT FROM THE FACT THAT VALIANT IS A WELL-TRIED AND PROVEN CAR. Right from its introduction in the U.S.A. in 1959, Valiant won unstinted applause from the public and motoring critics alike. Now Valiant comes to Australia, proved and improved as the result of the experience in the hands of over 500,000 owners.

2. TO SAY THAT YOU WILL BE THRILLED AT THE WAY THIS CAR HANDLES IS AN UNDERSTATEMENT. If you haven't driven Valiant, please take that test drive soon. As for its all-round qualities of performance, we are content to let Valiant speak for itself.

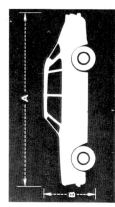

3. YOU'LL BE PROUD TO DRIVE THE LONGEST, LITHEST BEAUTY IN ITS CLASS. You don't need a tape-measure to confirm this fact, your eyes (and pulse) will tell you it is so. Valiant's dimensions are: (a).**Overall length,** 184.2 in.: (b) Overall height (unladen). 56.7 in.

VALIANT

In the field of medium-priced "sixes" Chrysler has the last word with...

If you have been in the habit of going back, year after year, to the same make of medium-priced car, here is the newcomer that will really tempt you to change your mind . . . VALIANT . . . so new, it is unlike any other car you have ever driven.

With you behind the wheel, Valiant can actually write its own sales story on the road. You can positively *feel* the dramatic difference in its ultra-modern, 30° slanted engine . . . the incredible smoothness and stability of Valiant's "TorsionAire ' ride and wider tracks. In so many other ways, too, such as the quietness of Unibody construction and the convenience of the battery-saving alternator, you see and sense that Valiant is different and better.

From now on, when considering a medium-priced car, you owe it to yourself to make a critical assessment of all "three". . . and particularly to drive them. As far as Valiant is concerned, you won't be given any long drawn-out sales talk . . . it won't be necessary . . . not when Valiant can change your mind all by itself!

...STRUCTION ENDS THE MAJOR CAUSE OF BODY RATTLES AND SQUEAKS. Instead of bolting body to frame, Valiant combines both into a rigid one-piece unit by over 5,300 spot and seam welds.

"The Autocar" described Chrysler's "Unibody" as "the most advanced unit-construction body yet designed".

...reason why Valiant is so sure footed is its wide track, 55.9 in. at front, 55.6 in. at rear.

4. YOU WILL APPRECIATE VALIANT'S "KING-SIZE" LUGGAGE SPACE (BIGGEST IN ITS CLASS). Valiant's luggage boot is 50.2 in. long, capacity 24.9 cu. ft., and every square inch is usable because the spare tyre is completely out of the way—flat mounted in a special recessed compartment in the floor.

5. STYLE THAT WILL MAKE YOU STOP, LOOK AND WHISTLE. The natural colour photos of Valiant shown in this catalogue speak more convincingly than a thousand words.

6. YOU'LL FIND CHRYSLER "TORSION-AIRE" THE SMOOTHEST RIDE OF YOUR LIFE. Instead of coil springs at the front, Valiant has torsion bars of high-chrome steel. The torsion (or twist) of these bars resists the up-and-down motion of the wheels, gradually, giving you a smoother, steadier ride.

At the rear are wide-spaced, fast-acting "Levelizer" leaf springs. These are made stiff near the front for firm ride control, limber at the back for gentle cushioning.

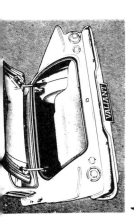

11. INSTRUMENTS ARE EASY TO READ. Instruments are grouped in front of the driver in a hooded panel, matt-black in colour to eliminate reflections.

12. FRONT SEAT "TAILORS" ITSELF TO SUIT YOUR DRIVING POSITION. Mounted on a curved track, the front seat tilts back slightly when moved to the rear.

8. ANOTHER CHRYSLER "FIRST"...THE AMAZING NEW ALTERNATOR. Unlike the generator, Valiant's alternator keeps charging even when the engine is idling. The result—easier starting in cold weather, less battery trouble and longer battery life.

9. OPTIONAL TORQUEFLITE 3-SPEED, PUSH-BUTTON AUTOMATIC TRANSMISSION. TorqueFlite is a completely automatic 3-speed transmission, controlled by the accelerator pedal and five pushbuttons. All upshifts or downshifts are made automatically and quietly. Pushbutton D (drive) covers all normal driving needs. Pressing the "2" button keeps transmission from shifting to "high", providing powerful engine braking, or for stop-and-go driving in heavy traffic. Button "1" holds transmission in low range for driving in sand or mud. A lever is provided to lock the transmission when parked.

lbs./ft. torque. It performs like a V8, but has the traditional economy of a "six".

14. DUAL HEADLIGHTS. Look smarter, provide greater safety for night driving.

15. VISIBLY, VALIANT PUTS SAFETY FIRST. Wide, curved windscreen and low bonnet line give a clear view of the road ahead.

16. PERFECT PROTECTION IN CASE OF A BLOW-OUT. Valiant has 14-in. Safety Rim Wheels, another Chrysler "exclusive".

17. REVERSING LIGHTS STANDARD EQUIPMENT. Greater safety at night.

18. SCREENED COWL-TOP VENTILATING SYSTEM. Extra comfort in hot weather.

19. SAFETY-PADDED INSTRUMENT PANEL.

20. LONGER PERIODS BETWEEN ENGINE OIL CHANGES—Now only necessary every 4,000 miles.

21. SAVINGS THROUGH SIMPLIFIED CHASSIS LUBRICATION. Major chassis lubrication now necessary only every 32,000 miles or two years. Number of lubrication points also substantially reduced by pre-lubrication and sealing at the factory.

13. THIS ENGINE WILL GIVE YOU A NEW SLANT ON POWER WITH ECONOMY. Valiant's ultra-modern O.H.V. "six" is inclined 30° to the right. This not only allows for a lower bonnet line, but also allows the water pump to be mounted on the side, saving 4 in. in engine length, which has been added to the passenger compartment. Inclining the engine also makes possible intake and exhaust manifolding of very high efficiency. The intake manifold has six individual branches which not only feed an even fuel mixture to each cylinder, but have long radius curves permitting gases to enter the cylinders with a minimum of restriction. Aluminium is used extensively to eliminate dead weight. Engine develops 145 B.H.P. and 215

DRIVE IT

feel the amazing difference!

TORSION BARS

VALIANT SPECIFICATIONS

DIMENSIONS: Wheelbase, 106.5 in.; Overall length, 184.2 in.; Overall width, 70.4 in.; Overall height, 55 in. (laden); Track—front, 55.9 in., rear, 55.6 in.; Ground clearance (laden), 7.0 in. **Weights:** 2,704 lbs. (std. trans.); 2,710 lbs. (automatic).

ENGINE: 6 cyl. in line, O.H.V. inclined 30°; bore, 3.40 in.; stroke, 4.125 in. Piston displacement, 225 cu. in.; Compression ratio, 8.2 to 1; Taxable horsepower, 27.7; Max. B.H.P., 145 @ 4,000 R.P.M.; Max torque (lb./ft.), 215 @ 2,800 R.P.M.

Combustion chambers are the in-line, wedge-shaped type, with large valves for efficient engine breathing. Exhaust valves have four bead-keepers, helping valves rotate, distributing wear evenly. Pistons, lightweight, tough aluminium alloy with two compression and one oil control ring. Crankcase ventilating system is closed type with flow-control valve, which gives back-fire protection and eliminates air pollution.

Single downdraft carburettor is calibrated to supply the exact fuel mixture for economical performance. Small diameter carburettor throat exercises better control of the fuel-air mixture. Automatic choke. Replaceable element air cleaner.

BODY CONSTRUCTION: All steel, full-unit construction. Welded-in front fender side shields, integral rear-quarter panels. Body is reinforced with heavy steel box-section girders. Two bolted-on structural "frame" members are used—the front K-section suspension cross member and the engine rear support cross member. Body has four doors, is fully dust, water and rust proofed, and extremely well insulated. Very special measures are taken to guard the underbody and similar exposed sections against corrosion. Body side sills are galvanised steel for added corrosion resistance.

TRANSMISSION: Manual—Dry plate clutch, total effective area 77.8 sq. ins. Release bearing, sealed ball bearings, permanently lubricated gearbox, three forward speeds, gear ratios 1st, 2.95 to 1; 2nd, 1.83 to 1; 3rd, 1.00 to 1; Reverse, 3.50 to 1. Synchromesh on 2nd and 3rd.

TRANSMISSION (Push-button, three-speed TorqueFlite Automatic): The TorqueFlite transmission combines a torque converter and an automatic planetary gearbox. The torque converter extends torque multiplication over a wide range of engine speeds. The automatic gearbox is controlled by hydraulic pressure supplied by the front and rear oil pumps; this pressure varies according to the throttle opening.

Depending on the drive range selected, the throttle opening and the car speed, the control valves will cause hydraulic pressure to engage or release the clutches and apply or release the bands, thus causing the planetary gear sets to provide three forward and one reverse ratio.

Gear ratio and gears used in each selected position:

"R"—reverse gear: 2.2 to 1 ratio.

"N"—neutral.

"D"—1st, 2nd and drive: 2.45, 1.45 and 1.00 to 1.

"2"—1st and 2nd: 2.45, 1.45 to 1.

"1"—1st: 2.45 to 1.

A lever is incorporated to lock the transmission when your Valiant is parked.

FUEL TANK: Capacity 11.7 Imp. Gals.

REAR AXLE: Semi-floating, hypoid, 2 pinion differential; composite construction with integral carrier. Ratio, 3.23 to 1.

BRAKES: Duo-servo, internal expanding; self-energising, centrifuse, cast-iron brake drums, diameter 9 in.; Effective lining area, 153.5 sq. ins. Moulded asbestos linings; Handbrake—T-handle, pull-on-type, located under instrument panel, right of steering wheel. Operates on rear wheels.

WHEELS AND TYRES: Disc, pressed steel, safety type rims, size—14 x 4.5J. Tyres (standard)—Five x 5.90 x 14, 4-ply tubeless.

SUSPENSION: Front—Heavy-duty, with independent lateral, non-parallel, unequal length control arms and torsion-bar springs. Rear: Heavy-duty, parallel, semi-elliptic longitudinal leaf springs. Double-acting shock absorbers front and rear.

STEERING: Linkage—Symmetrical idler arm, equal length tie rods. Steering-gear type, worm and recirculating ball. Turning circle, 36.4 ft.

EQUIPMENT: Adjustable ventilating front quarter windows; Ash trays for front and rear passengers; two adjustable sun visors, one with vanity mirror; Arm-rests on all doors; Reversing lights; Cigar lighter; Flashing turn signal lights with indicator light on instrument panel; Dome lamp operated by head-light switch and door courtesy switches; Dual horns; Instrument panel with speedometer, odometer, fuel gauge, water temperature gauge, ammeter and oil pressure indicator light.

TWELVE MONTHS OR 10,000 MILES WARRANTY

OPTIONAL EQUIPMENT

FOR YOUR ADDED PLEASURE AND CONVENIENCE . . .

Valiant is very well equipped for your driving pleasure. However, many people like to add individual touches to their cars, so MoPar provides a very fine range of specially tailored accessories for your Valiant.

POWER BRAKES
PUSH-BUTTON RADIO
RADIO REAR-SHELF SPEAKER
FOOT-OPERATED SCREEN WASHER
EXTERIOR REAR-VIEW MIRROR
LUGGAGE COMPARTMENT LAMP
HEATER AND DEMISTER KIT
"DAY-NITE" INTERIOR MIRROR
WHEEL TRIM RINGS
EXTERIOR SUN VISOR
LOCKING FUEL CAP
REAR WINDOW VENETIAN BLIND
DOOR WEATHER SHIELD
SAFETY BELTS

The policy of Chrysler Australia Limited is one of continual improvement in design and manufacture, wherever possible to assure a still finer car. Hence, specifications, equipment and prices are subject to change without notice.

CHRYSLER AUSTRALIA LIMITED, ADELAIDE, S.A.

AP5 SERIES (1963)

By late 1962 Chrysler Australia Ltd had begun an 18 million pounds expansion plan to lift production to 50 000 units per year by 1967.

By 1963 Chrysler was building Valiants in Australia instead of merely assembling them. The company had started stamping panels and making dies and was working on ambitious new facilities at Tonsley Park in South Australia.

On 30 May that year a new model was released, based on the US Valiant but considerably modified for local conditions. In fact, the new model was so 'Australianised' that it shared only six body panels with its US counterpart. This, the AP5, looked markedly different from its predecessor but carried over most mechanical features.

Despite enough local input for the model to be recognised as the first 'Aussie Valiant', the engines were imported as was most sheet metal forward of the windscreen. The idea of using US panels at the front was to allow the Australian operation to stamp the rear panels while taking advantage of any US facelifts at minimal expense.

The AP5 was a similar width to the previous model but slightly longer. Its styling was more in line with the contemporary Holden and Falcon than that of the R or S Series.

The AP5 used the same 3.6-litre 225 'Slant Six' engine as previous models but had a new single-barrel, downdraft Holley carburettor which retained the 109 kw (145 bhp) output while slightly improving the fuel economy.

The suspension was largely unchanged, although softer springs were fitted to the rear.

The AP5's Australianisation included a unique extruded aluminium grille, a larger boot than the US model, a different rear deck and a flat rear window. Chrysler claimed a 12 per cent improvement in body torsional stiffness.

The AP5 had only two headlights instead of the previous model's four. The interior trim was a two-tone synthetic material and there was more padding in the seats than in previous models. Such 'extras' as sun visors, cigar lighters and ashtrays topped a fairly modest standard equipment list.

A special version — the Regal — was released to compete with the luxury Holden Premier and Falcon Futura. The Regal had more body decoration than the standard

The first Valiant to roll off the Tonsley Park assembly line — a white AP5 sedan — is inspected by Chrysler Australia's managing director David Brown and visiting Chrysler executive Irving Minett (left).

Valiant, better seats, automatic transmission and other features as standard.

Identified by its bonnet and boot emblems, whitewall tyres and distinctive wheel trims, the Regal was equipped with interior carpets, a two-tone steering wheel, fold-down armrests and contoured individual seat squabs covered with what was described as 'rich sponge vinyl trim'.

The new Valiant model line-up was very well received by the press which, while mildly begrudging the less spectacular appearance of the new model, generally complimented its smooth lines. They also praised the performance and 'roadability'.

The waiting list became longer, not only because of the Valiant's growing reputation but because there was a price drop from the old model. This amounted to 35 pounds for the manual and 40 pounds for the automatic.

The new prices were 1220 pounds ($2440) for the manual, 1345 pounds ($2690) for the automatic and 1498 pounds ($2996) for the Regal.

In November 1963 'Safari' station wagon variants were added to the range in manual, automatic and Regal form. Priced from 1320 pounds ($2640), the wagons used the same mechanical components and front-end styling as the sedans but were fitted with bigger tyres and heavier rear springing.

The main selling features were the enormous rear luggage space, the low-level counterbalanced tailgate, and a wind-up rear window which could be locked in any position.

A total of 49 440 AP5 Valiants was built.

AP5 Safari wagon.

wheels ROAD TEST

TECHNICAL DETAILS
OF THE
CHRYSLER VALIANT

SPECIFICATIONS

ENGINE:

Cylinder	six, in-line, inclined 30 deg to right
Bore and stroke	3.4 by 4.125 in
Cubic capacity	3688 cc
Compression ratio	8.2 to 1
Valves	pushrod, overhead
Carburettor	single, downdraught
Power at rpm	145 bhp at 4000 rpm
Maximum torque	215 ft lb at 2400 rpm

TRANSMISSION:

Type "Torqueflyte" three-speed auto, push-button operated

SUSPENSION:

Front	independent, by torsion bars
Rear	solid axle, long half-elliptic springs
Shockers	telescopic

STEERING:

Type	recirculating ball
Turns, L to L	five
Circle	39 ft 5 in

BRAKES:

Type	drum

DIMENSIONS:

Wheelbase	8 ft 10 in
Track, front	4 ft 7.9 in
Track, rear	4 ft 7.6 in
Length	16 ft 4½ in
Width	5 ft 9 in
Height	4 ft 7 in

TYRES:

Size	5.90 by 14

WEIGHT:

Kerb	24 cwt

PERFORMANCE

TOP SPEED:

Fastest run	90.9 mph
Average all runs	90.2 mph

MAXIMUM SPEED IN GEARS:

Low	47 mph
Intermediate	74 mph
Drive	90.9 mph

ACCELERATION:

Standing quarter mile:

Fastest run and average	19.3 sec
0 to 30 mph	4.25 sec
0 to 40 mph	6.5 sec
0 to 50 mph	9.7 sec
0 to 60 mph	13.75 sec
0 to 70 mph	20.8 sec
0 to 80 mph	31.2 sec
20 to 40 mph	3.6 sec
30 to 50 mph	4.9 sec
40 to 60 mph	6.8 sec

GO-TO-WHOA:

0 to 60 to 0 mph	18.1 sec

SPEEDO ERROR:

Indicated	Actual
30 mph	32.1 mph
50 mph	50.3 mph
70 mph	69.2 mph

FUEL CONSUMPTION:

Overall for test (170 miles)	16.9 mpg

WHY FOLLOW THE LEADER...
DRIVE IT!

VALIANT
BY CHRYSLER

BRILLIANT VALIANTS

PROVIDE VARIETY FOR YOUR CHOICE-PLUS TOP VALUE

The pride of Leadership will be yours . . . unmistakably . . . in a Valiant. Know the thrill of owning the car that **started** ahead of all others in its class . . . and today, is even more firmly established as the Leader . . . Valiant, too, leads in Station Wagon design . . . ahead with fresh, fine fashion-setting lines—ahead with so many practical things that add to the sheer enjoyment of Station Wagon living . . . In every way, every Valiant offers everything to fit the Australian way of life . . Top value for money . . . Safety . . . Solidity . . . A vehicle that is broad shouldered and roomy . . . The full measure of power that's needed to cover long distances at a gallop . . . yet easy on the gallons . . . Now, to fit your family ways and means, Valiant provides the choice of six models—Valiant Sedan and Safari Station Wagon, each available with manual or TorqueFlite automatic transmission—The luxury Regal sedan and the superb Regal Safari Station Wagon—both, of course, equipped with TorqueFlite automatic transmission . . . But whichever you choose, you will enjoy the deepest satisfaction of owner-ship . . . Driving a sedan or station wagon that has no master on the road . . . except you.

VALIANT SEDAN - MANUAL TRANSMISSION
This model Valiant looks expensive . . . but really it's so easy to own. Priced competitively in its field—but offering so much more for the money. The room, the ride, the power, the safety—all the qualities that make you proudest to own Valiant.

TOP QUALITY – BY DESIGN!

VALIANT HAS THE PERFORMANCE THAT MAKES DRIVING EXCITING ALL OVER AGAIN.

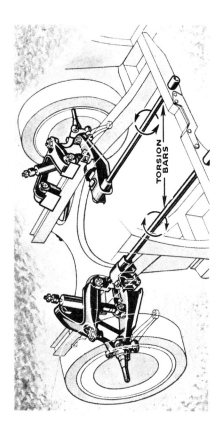

TORSION BAR FRONT SUSPENSION—ONE OF THE REASONS FOR VALIANT'S SMOOTH, STABLE RIDE. Torsion-bars ride better than coil springs because they react faster and bounce less. Combined with Valiant's modern front-end suspension geometry and balanced with special shock absorbers, Valiant's riding motion is level and gentle—no sudden lurch on corners—no sudden "nose-dive" with normal braking. You ride on velvet all the way. In Regal Safari and Safari, all these qualities are maintained through the use of special, heavier, station wagon suspension. Another reason why Valiant is so sure-footed is its wide front and rear tracks—Front track 55.9", rear 55.6". Good ground clearance, 7" with 3 passengers.

VALIANT'S 'LIFE PRESERVER' ...THE ALTERNATOR

Unlike the generator it obsoletes, Valiant's alternator keeps charging even when the engine is idling. The result, easier starting in cold weather, less battery trouble, longer battery life.

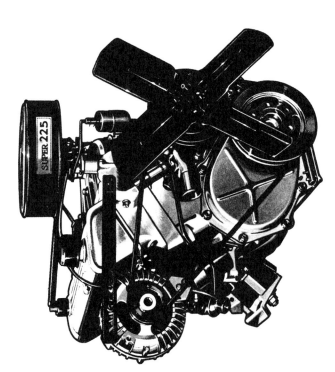

THIS IS THE ENGINE THAT GIVES YOU A NEW SLANT ON UNMATCHED PERFORMANCE WITH ECONOMY—Valiant's ultra-modern O.H.V. "Six" engine is inclined 30° to the right. This results in a low bonnet line and also allows the waterpump to be mounted on the side, which reduces overall engine length, the space saved being added to the passenger compartment. Slanting the engine also makes possible intake and exhaust manifolding of very high efficiency which contributes to Valiant's economy. Intake manifold has six individual branches which feed an even fuel mixture to each cylinder. Exhaust manifolds have long radius curves so that the expulsion of burnt gases is fast and complete. A crankshaft dynamic balancer adds to overall engine smoothness. The engine develops 145 B.H.P.@4,000 r.p.m. maximum torque 215 lbs. ft.@ 2,400 r.p.m.

BUILT "BY CHRYSLER" MEANS

MORE FOR YOUR MONEY WHEN YOU BUY . . . MORE WHEN YOU TRADE

AUTOMATICALLY . . . THE FINEST TRANSMISSION

TorqueFlite is the smoothest, most silent of all automatic transmissions, is simple in design, has no excess weight. It is a completely automatic, 3-speed transmission, controlled by the accelerator and 5 push buttons, which are illuminated at night. All upshifts and downshifts are made automatically, quietly. Push button "D" (drive) covers all normal driving needs. Push-button "1" (low) engages and holds first gear; is used for braking on steep grades. Push-button "2" keeps transmission from shifting to "high"; is ideal for driving in heavy traffic and provides jet-like acceleration. A lever is provided to engage transmission lock when parking.

VALIANT PUTS YOUR SAFETY FIRST

Apart from Valiant's amazing stability on the road—there are other factors which make this the most sure-footed car on the road—Big braking, for example; total effective braking area 153.5 sq. ins. Valiant is also fitted with Chrysler Safety-Rim wheels for added protection in case of sudden tyre damage.

26¾ CUBIC FEET OF LUGGAGE SPACE

This is yet another of the many ways in which Valiant and Regal Sedans give you much more. Just compare this boot size with anything else in the popular price field. Boot is long and high and wide, max. length 51½ inches—no trouble about stacking big cases here—every inch of space is clear loading space. Spare tyre concealed under boot floor. Boot lid counter-balanced. Floor covered with rubber mat. Valiant Regal boot mat is colored.

GOOD-BYE TO BODY RATTLES AND SQUEAKS FOR A LIFETIME

The Chrysler system of Unibody construction has been still further improved for added strength, quietness and even simpler construction. Every component and sheet metal panel is a functional part of the all-welded shell, ensuring maximum strength with minimum weight. The skin is a unified stressed component, sharing loads throughout the body. Tests have shown Valiant to have 12% greater twist-stiffness than the previous model. In addition, even greater attention has been paid to rust-proofing.

A STYLE WITH A PRACTICAL PURPOSE

Full width rear window of the sedans is only slightly off the vertical, providing undistorted rear vision and is less prone to catch and reflect on to the rear seat passengers the sun's rays during the hottest times of the day. The design of the rear quarter panels plus the use of massive centre door pillars help give the roof great structural strength.

IMPORTANT DETAILS

Reversing lights standard all models. Long-range fuel tank, 14.3 gallons. Low effort engine-hood latch. Printed circuits for instruments. Parallel action windshield wipers with a bigger field of operation. 2-speed electric windscreen wiper motor with ample power. Engine hood and deck lid counter-balanced by torsion bars; 14 in. safety road wheels.

SPECIFICATIONS IN BRIEF:

DIMENSIONS. Wheelbases 106"; Track—front 55.9", rear 55.6".

ENGINES. 225 Slant '6' Type, 6 in-line; O.H.V.; 30° inclined; Bore 3.40"; Stroke 4.125"; Displacement 225 cu. ins.; Compression ratio 8.4 : 1; B.H.P. at R.P.M. 145 at 4,000; Torque at R.P.M. 215 lb./ft. at 2,400; Taxable H.P. 27.7. **273 V8** Type 90° V8; Bore 3.63"; Stroke 3.31"; Displacement 273 cu. ins.; Compression ratio 8.8 : 1; Max. B.H.P. at R.P.M. 180 at 4,200; Max. torque at R.P.M. 260 lb./ft. at 1,600.

BRAKES. Duo-servo, self-adjusting, hydraulic. Power brakes and finned brake drums on the 273 V8.

SUSPENSION. Front—Independent, lateral, non-parallel control arms with torsion bars. Rear—Longitudinal leaf springs.

TRANSMISSION. Manual — 3-speed, synchromesh all forward ratios. **Automatic** — TorqueFlite 3-speed. Gear selector by quadrant and lever on steering column. For the 273 V8, gear selector in floor console.

WHEELS AND TYRES. Valiant 6.45 x 14 x 4 ply. Safari 6.95 x 14 x 4 ply. Valiant Regal 6.45 x 14 x 4 ply, white wall. Regal Safari 6.95 x 14 x 4 ply, white wall. 273 V8 Sedan and Safari 6.95 x 14 x 4 ply, low profile, white wall.

WARRANTY. 12 months or 12,000 miles.

CHRYSLER
AUSTRALIA LTD.

THE PROUDEST OWNERS WILL SIT RIGHT HERE.

Valiants are well equipped for your comfort and convenience. Windscreen washers are standard on all models. Ducted internal fresh air supply, two sun visors, visor vanity mirror, seat-belt anchorage points, full width instrument panel crash pad, arm rests all 4 doors, cigar lighter on instrument panel. Turn signal indicator has two arrows to indicate whether the right or left hand turn position has been engaged. Valiant Regal and Regal Safari, have, in addition, a heater/demister, Prismatic interior rear view mirror, dual rear-seat ashtrays, courtesy switches on all doors, seat arm rests. Valiant manual and automatic interior pictured above. Valiant Regal below.

AP6 SERIES (1965)

Released in March 1965, the AP6 was a development of the AP5 and a curtain raiser to the sensational AP6 V-8 to be released later in the year.

The AP6 featured the same basic bodywork as its predecessor but had an ornate split grille, slightly protruding headlights, a new bonnet and new front guards which made it 63 mm (2 inches) longer.

Several new technical features included self-adjusting brakes and an automatic transmission lever which was controlled by a quadrant and lever on the steering column. Gone were the push-button gears, which had never been popular (Chrysler claimed the change was made in response to a move to standardise gearshift operations across the industry).

A redesigned camshaft was fitted to the AP6 to improve torque by giving increased valve overlap and a higher lift action. Power brakes were available as a factory extra.

Acrylic enamel was introduced with the AP6 and metallic colours were offered for the first time. As with the AP5, two-tone trim was also available.

At the time of release, the model line-up was basically the same as with the AP5 — manual, automatic and Regal sedans, plus wagon variants. The Regal was identified by a broad chrome moulding along the side at mid height.

Praised by the media as 'quiet' and 'unusually powerful', the AP6 returned 12.8 L/100 km (22 mpg) around the city and 11.8 L/100 km (24 mpg) in the country in at least one test. Prices were unchanged, starting at 1240 pounds ($2480) and rising to 1625 pounds ($3250) for the Regal Safari.

In April Chrysler introduced the Valiant Wayfarer — an Australian-designed utility based on the Valiant sedan. It sold for 1059 pounds ($2118) in manual form and 1174 pounds ($2348) in automatic.

August brought the release of the first V-8 to be offered by the Big Three — the Valiant AP6 V-8. It was powered by a 4.4-litre (273 cubic inches) US-built engine developing 135 kW (180 bhp) and producing 352.6 Nm (260 lb ft) of torque.

The engine was the same as that used in the US Plymouth Barracuda and gave the Valiant a top speed of 175 km/h (109 mph).

The new V-8 model was available in sedan or wagon form, using the same basic bodies as the Sixes. It was distinguished by V-8 emblems on the front guards, boot lid and bonnet. The sedan version had a vinyl-covered steel roof (available in black or white) as standard; the Safari wagon came equipped with a roof-rack.

The three-speed 'TorqueFlite 8' transmission was standard on both models.

The V-8-engined AP6 was 57 kg (125 lbs) heavier than the standard model, and to cope with the additional power and weight, the rear suspension was stiffened and a heavy-duty 3.23:1 rear axle fitted. Power-assisted brakes were standard but no discs were offered. The front suspension remained unchanged.

The V-8 Valiant was priced at just under 1800 pounds ($3600).

At the time of the V-8 release, a Chrysler press release boasted:

'Valiant sedans, station wagons and utilities are being produced at the 18 million pounds Tonsley Park plant at the maximum rate of 200 units an eight-hour shift — but Chrysler still cannot meet its Australian demand.

'The current range, which now comprises ten Valiant models, has an Australian content of about 65 per cent, and this will be progressively increased to the Commonwealth Government's requested figure of 95 per cent in less than five years.'

43 344 AP6 Valiants were made.

ABOVE: New round tail-lights were fitted to the AP6 Safari wagon.

LEFT: The Regal interior. Note new auto gearshift.

BELOW: The Wayfarer Utility.

*Slung into a downhill right-handed hairpin the Valiant kneels some and lifts a front wheel in **understeer**, but remains quite stable.*

VALIANT'S VIRILE 8

The three faces of the new Mopar: It's fine for going down to the supermarket, good enough for the managing director, and just about right for the drag strip. But it's still just a V8 compact, after all.

So much has already been said and written about the Chrysler Valiant V8 that it is difficult to readjust oneself to taking a fresh approach to the car. This is probably because most of the motoring journalists who have tested the car and written about it have regarded the V8 as a new and exciting boost to what is essentially one of the fairly dull six-cylinder cars that dominate the Australian market. However, from another angle you find that Chrysler has, in effect, simply marketed the sort of V8 compact car that has been selling consistently in America for the last three years. Apart from minor differences in styling and slight alterations in engineering and local conditional proofing, this is no street fireball, but merely the sort of car that millions of American moms use to trundle down to the supermarket or pick

WHEELS **FULL ROAD TEST**

*V8 Valiant uses Regal brightwork, but can be identified by
V8 badges on bonnet, flanks and boot, as well as new vinyl top.*

*Above: The 273 cubic inch V8 fits neatly into engine
bay. Everything is surprisingly accessible. Note brake
servo and washer tank at left, alternator at centre.*

*Right: Stick shift for automatic transmission is well-
placed, easy to use. Individual seats are a little firm,
but good and wide, and carpeting is of good quality.*

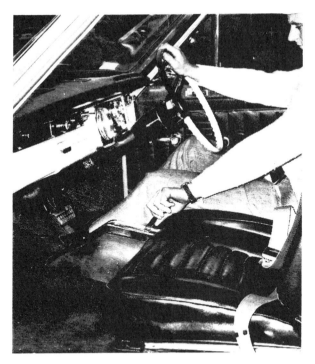

up the kids from school.

In Australia it is a luxury car by reason of price
and the hot dog trim which Chrysler Australia has
installed in it; but by anybody's standards this is not
a high-performance car. It is not particularly fast,
the 273 cubic inch V8 is not (at 4474 ccs, certainly)
the bellowing, fire-breathing monster our six cylinder
minds think it to be, and the Valiant V8 certainly
does not deserve the aura of fearsome power that

some journalists have given it and which the Road
Safety Council seems to think will increase the road
toll overnight.

No, the Valiant V8 is simply a well-balanced compact with luxury trim and adequate power. No more,
no less. Chrysler has done a good job of engineering
it, apart from the lack of braking ability, and in the
40-70 mph speed ranges where so much Australian
motoring is done this car is infinitely safer than its

six-cylinder brother because of the extra power.

We tend to forget that the V8 has only 35 bhp more than the slant six, and the car weighs some 150 lb more, so the raw power-to-weight ratio is not all that startlingly different. However, a V8 engine produces proportionately more torque over a wider range, and this gives smoothness and flexibility that make the car a far better proposition for the prestige or luxury buyer. It also mates better to an automatic transmission than a six.

Thus one would expect that using a 273 cubic inch V8 in a luxury Valiant would give you a well-balanced, quiet and effortless prestige car. We think that Chrysler has succeeded in this, with the exception of the brakes, the problem of using locally-made

"normal" tyres on a car capable of getting to 100 mph in any reasonable stretch of road, and the difficulty of getting a trimmed-up Valiant to look like anything more than a trimmed-up Valiant. However, we've said it before, and it bears repeating: This car represents the start of a new era in the Australian motor industry. The V8 is with us to stay.

Chrysler engineers at the Sydney press conference to announce the car went to great lengths to stress that it had not been a case of simply dropping the V8 in the slant six engine bay. The extra engineering has gone into the front suspension, steering geometry, transmission and soundproofing. The steering has been made lighter, helped by positioning the shorter V8 further rearward in the engine bay and getting some weight off the front wheels. The result has been that at 4.75 turns lock to lock (Chrysler claims four) the steering is quite nicely geared, and at 37 ft the turning circle is not excessive.

The attention to soundproofing has been quite successful, for very little engine noise gets back to the occupants, apart from what is now a typical Chrysler V8 fan belt whistle. Even when spun right out in the intermediates by using the manual lock-in on the automatic transmission the little V8 does not thrash or roar. It has a great deal of punch low down; we found that by hanging the car up on the footbrake at about 3000 rpm for a standing start we could spin the wheels readily for perhaps 15 ft. This, by the way, is not recommended as normal traffic light procedure — we used it only to record standing start acceleration figures. If the driver floors the throttle while sitting there at an idle the car will just whisk off the line like a jack-rabbit.

We found very little difference in acceleration times by using Drive range or the manual lock-in, which was only slightly faster. This indicates just how much of the V8's torque is developed low in the range, for holding the transmission in each gear gave us only 7 mph more in first and 19 mph more in second. However, because second can be held up to 81 mph, where valve crash starts to be felt rather than heard, acceleration between 50 and 80 mph is very good. It was interesting, incidentally, that on this test car — white with black vinyl roof — the speedometer was slightly fast to 50 mph when it became that rare thing — a little slow.

(Continued on page 78)

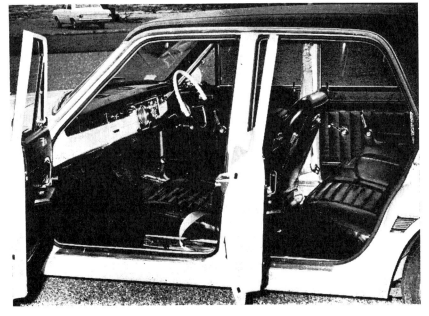

Leg room in rear with front seats right back is more than adequate. Head room is also good. There are coathooks in the rear.

All-black interior gives that essential luxury touch, while the car is very comfortable for five people. Note centre armrest.

VALIANT'S VIRILE 8

(Continued from page 26)

At 70 mph we were actually doing 71.2 mph.

Wildly optimistic top speed figures for this car are fairly common (the habit was probably started by another magazine crew which drove a dealer's car with nought miles and proceeded to estimate top speed as well in excess of 110 mph). The V8 has too much frontal area and too long a "tail" in the torque curve to get anywhere near this. Standing quarter-mile times are very good, however. Our companion magazine HOT-RODDING managing to squeeze the car down to 16.6 by using drag-strip tricks, so the potential is there.

The Valiant V8 is interesting for yet another thing — the straight line shifter installed to operate a strengthened TorqueFlite three-speed automatic torque converter transmission. The gate is covered with a sliding panel that follows the movements of the stick, which is topped by a large black ball with thumb-sized indents at each side. It is a hefty affair, very masculine-looking and moves very silently and smoothly. Too smoothly in some cases, for while there are positive stops going from drive to second and first there are none on the way back up; if you shift manually from second to drive you can easily overrun into neutral. Reverse and park, at the top (front) end of the shift line, are suitably gated off, however.

AMPLE TORQUE

Normally you leave the thing in drive and it just swishes along, upshifting and downshifting in all the right places without ever letting the driver know it is working. On a very light throttle you can fetch drive at less than 20 mph, but there is ample torque there to take care of things. The throttle kickdown detent operates at just below 35 and 60 mph — the normal upshift points in drive range.

Handling is better than that of the Valiant six, simply because lightening the steering has taken away some of that truckie's feel. The suspension changes are too slight to account for the improved way this car can be slung into corners, for the understeer is there in the same amount. The steering is just nicer, that's all. There is very little feed-back on rough roads, although some slight body panel tremble, and you can provoke wheel hop by trying very hard. On tightish bitumen corners taken hard there is a lot of front-end ploughing and we even managed to get an inside front wheel off the ground in places. But this is at velocities which the normal V8 prestige-type owner would not dream of attempting.

TYRE SQUEAL

The ride has not altered very much, remaining that fairly typical Chrysler torsion bar ride which is slightly firmer than that of coil springs but less resistant to fore-and-aft pitching in extremes while minimising lateral roll movement. The result is good travel over most surfaces, with faint front wheel shimmy over corrugations and a touch of thumping over concrete road expansion seams. But the noise transference is low, despite "normal" tyre tread patterns, although this could certainly be due to extra soundproofing and heavy carpeting. The built-in understeer causes a fair amount of tyre squeal, but some fiddling with the pressures enabled our crew to cut down the understeer a bit and quieten the tyres somewhat.

About the only item not in keeping with the car's smooth and strong nature is the braking system. Chrysler claims a lot for the finned drums it has put on the V8, and the car certainly stops a little better than the slant six, which (in our test cars at least) suffered from interminable wheel locking and unpredictable fade, as well as some weaving in 0.75 g stops from high speed. The V8 stops neatly and cleanly most of the time, but you can fade the brakes in, say, a three-mile mountain descent. However, the fade is limited in extent, and recovery is surprisingly rapid.

We did not, however, particularly like the car on wet roads. Despite a fairly high 3.23 final drive gearing, a careless driver can easily provoke wheel-spin at 40 mph in drive. We also were not happy about continued high speed on the locally-made tyres (not only those on the test car but also those from the other original equipment tyre suppliers) simply because the tyre makers themselves will admit that these covers are not designed for sustained speeds of 90-100 mph.

Essentially the body of the V8 is the same as the six-cylinder car, apart from tastefully-done V8 emblems on boot lid, both flanks and as a bonnet emblem. However, it has the vinyl roof and black trim that is going to be so popular from now on; but you will have to be careful of your color combinations. Our test car, in black-and-white, looked marvellous.

The boot is carpeted, and the interior carries high-grade full carpeting in black. Upholstery is in first-class black Doehide, with more black highlights across the width of the facia. Instead of the Regal-type split bench with folding armrest fitted to the V8 wagon the sedan has two individual seats. These are quite wide and deep and heavily pleated horizontally. We found them to be a shade too firm for most of our test drivers. If they were a bit softer the good shape of the seats would automatically give one better sideways support. Also, Chrysler claims the seats have adjustment for rake, but we didn't find it on the test car. The back rests on that seemed to be fixed for life. It is also hard to wedge a hand between the seat cushion and the door to use the adjustment lever.

OVAL WHEEL

Door trimming is nicely done, with the material carried right up to the window sills and finished off with a V8 emblem. There is a folding centre armrest in the rear seat. On the test car the steering wheel — slightly oval for all V8s — was half black and half white. Well, perhaps. The seats give the driver a good angle of attack at the wheel, and there is enough rearward adjustment for six-footers.

Instrumentation is the same as in the normal Valiant, using one large dial for the speedometer and three smaller ones for fuel, oil pressure and water temperature. In addition there is a foot-operated washer button where the dipswitch should be, and a very efficient heater/demister unit controlled by sliding levers set a little too far away in the centre of the facia. The dipswitch is under the footbrake, a piece of design foolishness which went out with button-up boots, or so we had thought.

CRAZY DIPSWITCH

The standard of finish overall is quite good, but we personally would expect a little more equipment for our almost-£1800. The design of the demister vents seems unnecessarily "square", and the expanse of painted metal on the facia gets a bit oppressive. However, all the door hardware is suitably strong and t door armrests are in the right place. So there. There are ashtrays in the rear of each individual seat squab.

The V8 retains some of the Valiant's basic faults, like annoying wind roar at speed, fiddly quarter vent locks, and that crazy dipswitch, but it has also eliminated a lot of others.

In the final analysis, Chrysler has put together a well-integrated unit that handles the V8 very well and which will undoubtedly appeal to most of the already prestige-minded Valiant crowd. It will also certainly steal a few buyers from the Premier-Fairmont area, and may do this strongly enough to convince Ford and GM-H that the V8 is not just another rich man's toy. It has many advantages over the six, notably in the way it confers the impression of silent, effortless travel which we — like the Americans — are beginning to demand in our volume cars. The disadvantages are very poor fuel consumption, despite a relatively small two-barrel carburettor on the 273, higher initial cost, and the resistance of the "anti-speed" pressure groups which seem to thrive in our climate. We haven't heard the last of the in-lines, but there's a lot more to come from the bents. #

TECHNICAL DETAILS
OF THE
VALIANT V8

SPECIFICATIONS

ENGINE:
Cylinders .... Eight, in 90 degree Vee
Bore and stroke .... 3.63 in. (92.2 mm)
by 3.31 in. (84.0 mm)
Cubic capacity .... 273 cu in. (4474 ccs)
Compression ratio .... 8.8 to 1
Valves .... pushrod, overhead
Carburettor .... Carter 2-barrel downdraft
Power at rpm .... 180 bhp (SAE) at 4200
Maximum torque .... 260 lbs/ft at 1600 rpm
Piston speed at max. bhp .... 2317 ft/min

TRANSMISSION:
Gearing .... 22 mph per 1000 rpm in Drive
Type .... 3-speed automatic
Gear lever location .... central console
Ratios, overall.
First 7.91
Second 4.68
Third 3.23
Final drive .... 3.23 to 1

SUSPENSION:
Front .... lateral control arms, torsion bars
Rear .... semi-elliptic leaf springs
Dampers .... telescopic

STEERING:
Type .... worm and ball nut
Ratio .... 24.7 to 1
Turns, 1 to 1 .... 4.75
Circle .... 37 ft

BRAKES:
Type .... hydraulic drum
Swept or rubbed area .... 254.5 sq ins.

DIMENSIONS:
Wheelbase .... 8 ft 10 in.
Track, front .... 4 ft 7⅞ in.
Track, rear .... 4 ft 7¾ in.
Length .... 15 ft 7⅞ in.
Width .... 5 ft 9 in.
Height (laden) .... 4 ft 7 in.
Fuel tank capacity (maker's figure) ...... 14.3 gals
Boot capacity (maker's figure) .... 26.5 cu ft

TYRES:
Size .... 6.95 by 14
Make on test car .... Goodyear G8

WEIGHT:
Kerb (with fuel and water) .... 2957 lbs

GROUND CLEARANCE:
Laden .... 7 in.

PERFORMANCE

TOP SPEED:
Fastest run .... 108.4 mph
Average of all runs .... 104.8 mph

MAXIMUM SPEED IN GEARS:
First .... 42 mph
Second .... 81 mph
Drive .... 105 mph

TAPLEY PULL:
First .... off scale
Second .... 530 lbs/ton
Third .... 370 lbs/ton

ACCELERATION:
Standing quarter mile:
Fastest run .... 17.2 secs
Average of all runs .... 17.4 secs
0 to 30 mph .... 3.7 secs
0 to 40 mph .... 6.1 secs
0 to 50 mph .... 7.9 secs
0 to 60 mph .... 10.9 secs
0 to 70 mph .... 14.7 secs
0 to 80 mph .... 18.1 secs
20 to 40 mph .... 3.4 secs
30 to 50 mph .... 4.75 secs
40 to 60 mph .... 5.6 secs

SPEEDO ERROR:

Indicated	Actual
30 mph	29.3 mph
40 mph	39.1 mph
50 mph	50.5 mph
60 mph	60.8 mph
70 mph	71.2 mph
80 mph	81.2 mph

FUEL CONSUMPTION:
Overall for test .... 16.8 mpg
Normal cruising .... 15-18 mpg
Fuel used on test .... Super

TEST CONDITIONS:
Surface .... dry hot-mix bitumen
Weather .... fine, cool, strong wind

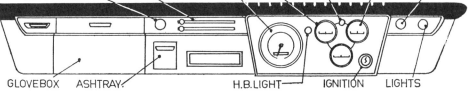

VC SERIES (1966)

VC Regal sedan.

The release of the VC Valiant in March 1966 stepped up the sales battle raging between the Big Three.

Some clever work from Chrysler's styling department made the new Valiant appear longer and lower, although it was essentially a facelifted version of the AP5/AP6 design. The overall dimensions were virtually unchanged.

Chrysler advertisements highlighted the new grille and front-end treatment and talked of 'bold imposing new styling' and 'up-to-the-minute sculpturing'.

The VC had deep-sectioned bumper bars with recessed park/turn signal lights. A new-look rear was created for the sedan with different panels and tail-lights, but the Safari wagon's tail remained similar to that of the previous model.

Along with the Safari wagon, the Wayfarer utility retained the previous exterior sheet metal except for the new bonnet and front guards.

The VC used the familiar 'Slant Six' engine. Nevertheless, the company claimed 'extensive mechanical refinements' which included a

new steering-column shift and a three-speed all-synchromesh gearbox. This was the first release of Borg Warner's Australian 'common industry' manual transmission. A new intrument panel was fitted to all new Valiants.

The VC series saw Chrysler attempting a more pronounced model definition, with greater variation in the exterior ornamentation and three distinct levels of interior trim.

The basic variants (Valiant, Regal and V-8) had individualised hubcaps, horn-rings and steering wheel motifs. The V-8 sedan still had the distinguishing touch of a black or white vinyl roof. The V-8 wagon acquired a chrome roof-rack and stainless steel air deflectors on each side of the tailgate. Their job was to keep grime off the tailgate glass.

Becoming more safety conscious, Chrysler fitted the Valiant with full-width instrument panel crash-padding, seat belt anchor points, safety door locks, a modified-zone windscreen, lift-up door handles, wide double-sided safety wheel rims, lower profile tyres and a larger glass area.

Weight was up about 36 to 45 kg (80 to 100 lbs) depending on the model.

Chrysler offered a higher equipment level with the VC. The base model listed such items as windscreen washers, dual-speed electric wipers, fresh air ventilation, vanity mirror, armrests on all doors, reversing lights, coat hooks, new-look floor mats and variable-intensity instrument lighting. A single chrome strip ran almost the length of the car.

The Regal and V-8 versions had these features plus heating and demisting equipment with a two-speed fan booster, full carpeting, central armrests, prismatic anti-glare rear-view mirror, boot light (sedan only), courtesy light switches on all doors, 'sponge vinyl' trim, door sill scuff plates, two-tone steering wheel, wheel trim-rings, dual horns, air deflectors on the station wagons and whitewall tyres.

The V-8 had new bucket seats with a full-length floor console plus a glove compartment and ashtray. The revised automatic transmission lever had a straight fore-and-aft selection with a push-button 'lock out' release for the pawl. On the Regal and V-8 models, the three-speed TorqueFlite automatic transmission was standard.

The utility had the lowest equipment level but this included an exterior rear-view mirror and a tonneau cover.

Metallic paint was available on the Regal and V-8. In late 1966 front disc brakes became optional.

Australia had changed to decimal currency (with 1 pound equalling 2 dollars) in February 1966 and the new models sold from $2490 for the basic manual sedan (up $10 from the previous model) to $3590 for the V-8 station wagon.

The manual ute cost $2128.

Interestingly, the VC Valiant was at this time the only Australian-made car freely available in Britain. The unusual trade set-up meant that the Brits could import a Valiant 20 000 km from Australia for $400 less than the cost of bringing a similar car the 6500 km distance from Detroit!

Despite this saving, the VC was not an enormous success in the small-car oriented UK, as it was considered too big for the narrow streets and congested parking arrangements.

In Australia it was a different story. The VC was well received and sales were excellent. The dream run hit a rough patch in March 1967, however, when for the first time, Valiant's position as the biggest-of-the-Big-Three was challenged.

In that month Ford released the Fairlane 500, based on the XR Falcon but with an extended wheelbase. At a time when bigger meant better, Ford's car was indeed better. And it came with a 150 kW (200 bhp) V-8!

The Valiant V-8 suddenly stopped being the top-of-the-pack. Worse still for Chrysler, Ford had made the V-8 available as an option on the Falcon range, meaning that while Chrysler

VC Wayfarer utility.

only offered the V-8 in one car, Ford gave V-8 performance in a smaller and a bigger car. And you didn't have to buy the top-line model to get it!

Ford had discovered how to play the options game and had saturated every price bracket between $2000 and $4000.

By early 1968 Valiant was in further trouble — GM-H had the 5-litre (307 cubic inches) Chevrolet V-8 available in its new HK Holden line-up.

This flood of V-8s caused a small rumbling about fuel consumption but manufacturers were quick to point out that Australian petrol was among the world's cheapest.

A complaint aired about the Valiant (which people didn't mention until the other V-8s turned up) was its noticeable understeer. Suddenly there were more fronts to fight on (and more front ends to fight against!).

65 634 VC Valiants were made before Chrysler launched the all-new VE.

The V-8 sedan and wagon.

Valiant

225 SLANT '6' AND 273 V8

Valiant has more to like than ever. A new, sleek symmetry of line that is the perfect blending of function, beauty and individuality . . . All the mechanical feature that have made Valiant the success it is, with each quality now developed to its highest degree of technical perfection. The well-proven 225 Slant '6' engine (nothing finer in its class), outstanding stability, ease of handling, riding smoothness, safety, and comfort. Valiant 225 available with manual transmission (now synchromesh on all forward ratios) or with TorqueFlite 3-speed automatic transmission. Valiant Regal 225 (photo front cover) has TorqueFlite standard, plus added luxury in trim and appointments.

VALIANT 225 (Manual or Automatic) & THE LUXURY VALIANT REGAL (Automatic)

Valiant Safari and Regal Safari are the station wagons that make every outing a pleasure, not a project. Power and safety to tow with ease a caravan or boat . . . Everything for station wagon living . . . Rear seat folds down in one single operation to give a full 7 feet of space between back of front seat and inside of tailgate . . . room to sleep in comfort or for all the gear you would ever want to carry. Tailgate is wide, sturdy and with low loading height. Safari station wagons are trimmed and equipped as their sedan counterparts. Regal Safari has front seat centre arm rest only. Air deflectors are mounted on the rear window pillars

VALIANT 225 SAFARI (Manual or Automatic) & LUXURY REGAL SAFARI (Automatic)

The 273 V8 is the top performing Valiant . . . and the most luxurious. In styling it has the clean-cut Valiant lines with subtle markings to denote the V8 model. In addition, a vinyl covered roof creates a dramatic styling note. Upholstery is in sponge vinyl. Doors are trimmed to full height. Front seats are contoured, thickly bolstered. Rear seat has folding centre arm rest. Floor and boot are carpeted. White wall tyres and de luxe wheel trims are fitted. Appointments are complete. The 273 V8 has the 3-speed TorqueFlite automatic with floor console gear selector. Added safety matches the higher performance. Brakes are big, power-assisted and have finned brake drums.

Valiant

225 SLANT '6' AND 273 V8

VALIANT 273 V8 & SAFARI V8

MAKE THE MOVE THAT MAKES THE DIFFERENCE.. MOVE UP TO VALIANT!

PERFORMANCE WITH SAFETY THAT LETS YOU ENJOY IT . . . VALIANT

Interior of the VC V-8 sedan.

VE SERIES (1967)

The VE Valiant V-8.

At the end of October 1967, Chrysler dodged the model designation of VD and released the all-new Valiant VE line-up — the most Australian Valiants to date.

The styling was an amalgam of Dodge Dart and US Valiant, with a long, low look and huge areas of almost flat sheet metal.

There were no carryover body panels from the VC except the floor plan which was considerably altered. The new models had a revised and more aggressive grille treatment, curved side glass, a concave rear window and a longer boot line.

The VE was bigger than earlier Valiants with the wheelbase increased by 50 mm to 2740 mm (108 inches), a wider track and the overall length up 140 mm (5 inches). It was much praised for its improved ride, better handling and bigger choice of options.

Chrysler Australia had been forced into the options race already underway between GM-H and Ford — and entered it with gusto.

The company's new weapon was the high-spec VIP model, fitted with the V-8 engine,

TorqueFlite automatic transmission, coaxial power steering (which according to the advertisements did '80 per cent of the work'), power-assisted front disc brakes and high-speed nylon cord tyres.

The VIP, however, was built on the same wheelbase as the standard Valiant, putting the new model at a distinct disadvantage against Ford's Fairlane.

By now there were no less than 18 Valiant variants. They used the base 'Slant Six' engine, a 120 kW (160 bhp) high-performance version of the 'Slant Six' and an improved version of the V-8.

Although the output of the 'Slant Six' fitted to the standard Valiant was still quoted at 109 kW (145 bhp), the engine had been modified for improved performance. A new carburettor and air cleaner were fitted and an exhaust system with lower back-pressure was added.

The 120 kW (160 bhp) high-performance engine was fitted as standard equipment to Regal models and the 109 kW (145 bhp) version was optional. By offering these choices,

Chrysler was attempting to plug up the big gaps in its price structure.

The 120 kW engine gained extra power from the use of a two-barrel carburettor with a matched-performance camshaft and a more efficient exhaust system.

This engine was optional for Valiant and Valiant Safari. When the high-performance engine was chosen, the vehicle was fitted with '100 mph rated' nylon-ply tyres.

The top-of-the-line engine, the V-8, was boosted to deliver 146 kW (195 bhp). Peak torque of 347 Nm (265 lb/ft) was produced at only 2000 rpm. This unit was standard on the VIP and VIP Safari and optional on the others.

The VE Valiant saw Chrysler become more serious about safety. All models featured dual line brakes, operated by a tandem master cylinder with separate front and rear braking systems. This was a first for a volume-produced Australian car.

As well as the much-publicised dual line brakes, the VE boasted such safety features as double-sided safety rim wheels, seat belts, greater all-round vision, exterior rear-view mirror on all models, a slightly modified suspension for improved roadholding, a recessed non-glare instrument panel, increased-power windscreen-wipers, electric windscreen washers, non-glare wiper arms and blades, padded sun visors, flush-fitting interior door handles and a shatterproof interior rear-view mirror.

The seat belts were a 'mandatory option', costing $10 on all models. Power-assisted front disc brakes were fitted to V-8 engine models and were optional on all others.

The new VIP model was lavishly furnished by the standards of the day. It had a cushioned transmission control console and individually adjustable reclining front bucket seats. These had 'dielectric impressions', allowing air to circulate around the body of the driver and passengers. The front seats had built-in adjustable headrests — a rare feature in 1967. Thick carpeting was fitted front and rear and in the boot.

The VIP Safari station wagon shared most of the same luxury specifications, plus a roof-rack, power-operated tailgate window and a rear interior dome light.

This new luxury flagship was extremely well received but did not completely escape criticism. At $3650 (for the sedan), some found the boot too shallow, the steering wheel too close to the driver and other controls not as well placed as they should be. Some details such as a vanity mirror, a speedometer tripmeter and rear reading lights were missing. It also lacked directional dashboard ventilation

The VE Safari.

outlets, a feature first seen in the 1962 Cortina but already becoming common.

Improvements added across the VE range included a 64-litre (14 gallons) fuel tank, a shorter gearlever throw on the manual gearbox, relocation of the dipswitch from under the brake pedal to the high left of the firewall and the changing of the windscreen washer system from vacuum to electric.

One reviewer said:

'The Valiant has always been quiet and the VE model maintains the tradition. Even the windscreen-wipers have lost their whine now that the motor is located on the other side of the firewall. Some road shock is felt up the steering columns but there is little suspension clatter.

'The Valiant is a very comfortable car for long trips and will appeal to the man who wants a large roomy and powerful car well below the prevailing prices for US-size vehicles.'

Several writers noted that they considered the VE Valiant the best handling car on bitumen, dirt and gravel then produced by the Big Three.

The Valiant price-list started at $2490, making its way to $3720 for the most expensive VIP wagon.

There were 68 688 VE Valiants made. During the production run, Chrysler reached its goal of 95 per cent (average) local content. The VE model had the distinction of being the first Valiant to win *Wheels* magazine's prestigious 'Car of the Year' award.

BELOW: The standard 225 Slant Six engine.
ABOVE RIGHT: The high-performance 225 Slant Six.
BELOW RIGHT: The 146 kW V-8.

New bodies, more power, more options in new VE Valiants, launched November 1. Brian Harman describes new range and road-tests 160 b.h.p. version of top-selling Valiant model

SQUARE speedo looks like old-fashioned radio dial: an odd touch in an otherwise modern dash layout with safely recessed controls. BELOW: Body is sleek, low (this is luxury Regal version).

MODERN MOTOR road TEST

CHRYSLER have moved out front in the Big Three horsepower race with uprated versions of the standard six cylinder engine and the V8 — but the extra power can be bought only with a safety equipment package.

Their new VE range for 1968 described in detail at the end of this story; we'll start by looking at what the extra neddies mean to the top selling Valiant model — the six cylinder automatic.

The pre-release 160 bhp automatic Valiant made available for **Modern Motor** to test in Adelaide was a bit short on miles but long on performance. It was very well screwed together and finished.

Apart from the $60 option of the hotter engine and the safety package complement of 100 mph tyres that must be included for the money, it had no other non-standard performance equipment except front disc brakes with power assistance that cost another $45. Price on the floor — $2835.

VALIANT EFFORT

No one in his right mind should imagine that the standard drum brakes will cope with the full performance of this anyman's firecracker

It casually blasted into orbit on the very crooked and dicey test track to the tune of 0-50 mph in 7.6 sec., caned the standing ¼-mile in 18.9 sec., and recorded a true top speed of 98.8 mph. First gear gave 38 mph, second 7? mph. The 40-60 mph bracket was swallowed up in 7.7 sec., the 50-7? mph in 8.5.

But the very good thing about the car is the way it handles and rides — and it isn't just due to the change to bigger tyres. Valiants have never impressed me with stick-downability at the back, although the torsion-bar set-up at the front has always been satisfactory. There has always too much power for the tyre area in contact with the road.

Now, if the VE is not the best handling car in the world, it is much more stable and the bigger tyres give it a chance. I would, though, like to see the D70 wide-treads standard on all models and not just on the VIP V8.

Even the 145 bhp bottom-of-the-line model could use them.

Main reason for the improved handling seems to me to be a bias of extra weight on the back wheels, which is probably as much a function of the longer wheelbase as the slightly softer suspension settings all round.

The test car understeered less, and on loose gravel tail breakaway was easily controlled by a flick of the steering. The back axle had better contact on poor roads and rough-surfaced corners.

There's still a bit of body roll, but it doesn't change the handling and ride is generally good—much better than it used to be in the rough.

Steering is unchanged at 4-plus turns lock-to-lock (I make it nearly five turns against the 4.4 claimed by the makers). When the co-axial power-steering is fitted (all the works except the pump are in the steering box, fed by oil pipes instead of being operated by Vee-belts), turns sensibly are cut to just under four. I tried a VIP and thought the application was good — some road feel is left except, strangely, at low speeds.

Torqueflite retained

The automatic Torqueflite is still the best in the business, the way it mates up with the 160 bhp engine — and the V8, for that matter. Up or down, heavy or light throttle, it pops in and out without any fuss at all, and quickly.

Steering-column selector positions are now laid out clearly — 1, 2, D, N, R, P — and the selector is precise and light. Position 1 engages first permanently, 2 does the same with second, D gives all three.

First peaked at 38 mph on throttle kickdown in D range and second gave a very useful 71 mph. The kickdown would bring either ratio in from the higher gear at 12 mph below those peak speeds.

Everyone who has sampled Torqueflite will be glad that it is with us to stay for the foreseeable future. Chrysler are going to take on Borg Warner, keeping only their torque-converter, in the interest of gaining local content. Now they have decided to get the whole of their transmission made here. This has cost a lot of dough,

GUARDS are so shaped that lights cannot be seen side on — black mark!

but I think they're dead right in protecting this big asset.

The power front brakes (the back brakes do NOT get power from the servo) kept the car steady under some pretty punishing runs on the test track and did not fade to any noticeable extent. This track was chosen by Chrysler for coyness about the new car being seen in more suitable places for testing. It was fine for bad-surface testing and couldn't have been better for the brakes, since all speed runs had to be made up to sharp corners not nearly far enough away from the ends of the quarter-mile. I was very glad when the session was over — although I had no chance to carry out the normal 10 crash stops program, I think the brakes got a worse hiding than if I had. They came through well.

The high-speed tyres were the new Uniroyal Tigerpaws with nylon casing, rated under the new standards set by the big tyre-makers as good for sustained running up to 100 mph and for up to 110 mph in short bursts (the precise definition of a short burst is 110 mph for not more than 10 minutes, and sustained speed means 100 mph for more than 10 minutes but not beyond one hour).

They held on well over smooth, dry bitumen and on the loose stuff. I had no chance to try them in the wet, and of course can make no comment on wearing qualities.

One thing, though — they did not suffer from the usual flat-spotting after a long stop (the wheels feel as if they're square for the first few miles on starting off of a morning) that so many nylon tyres do. Uniroyal claim that a new process of pre-stretching the nylon fibres in manufacture cuts this out.

Any fully run-in 160 bhp Valiant will be a true 100 mph car. Mine had only a bit over 400 miles on the clock and still bettered 98 mph. I would hate to have to rely on drum brakes, which are not mandatory with the safety package. This is not good enough, and neither is charging for front safety belts as an extra.

If Chrysler had made both these

items standard on all models, I think the rationalisation of option combinations could well have paid for them.

Body, interior

The new body — all question of taste aside — is not an unqualified success. The 108-in. wheelbase is not that long, and despite its extra 2in. length the inside seems no roomier than before.

In front there's no shortage of room and great wide doors, but the seat cushions are pitifully short, offering no thigh support.

The back doors are very narrow, knee-room just so-so, and again there's that miserable short cushion. Also, the wheel arches stick right into the compartment and the back of the seat is heavily curved and skimpily padded at each end. Certainly the back seat is not as good as before.

The standard seats — bench back and front — are comfortably upholstered. Regal and VIP models have better-quality stuff and fold-down armrests front and back.

The driving position will be quite comfortable for most sizes and shapes. The wheel could be a bit farther away for a tall driver's taste.

Instruments now surround a square speedo — the usual ones, minus oil-pressure gauge. The dash is padded deeply across the top and all controls are recessed — the cigarette lighter even has been tucked away inside the ashtray. Good layout.

Boot is appreciably bigger and useful in shape. Spare is buried, but the fuel filler pipe — such a nuisance in so many cars these days—is neatly out of the way, due to a double curve in it. I only hope it will take full flow from a bowser. The tank holds 14 gallons, which disappeared at the rate of 18.7 miles per gallon on the short and vicious test. Twenty should easily be come by in more normal use.

The one aspect of styling that can be criticised is that the body shape at each end carefully hoods back and front lights, so that the whole light sources are cut off from view by traffic

TAIL of new super-luxury VIP model, distinguished outwardly by badge on boot lip. Differences inside include headrest for driver, visible through huge back screen.

STRIFE on a loose dirt corner, through trying too hard for the camera — the 1968 VE model Valiant on our pre-release test near Adelaide. A handsome beast with many mechanical improvements, stacks of performance and good handling. BELOW LEFT: Luxury versions look fine inside but seating isn't all it could be. RIGHT: New twin-choke carby extracts more power.

VE Safari wagon sets a puzzle: it costs $200 more than sedan in standard Regal versions, only $70 more in VIP range.

approaching from the sides. What price safety?

Otherwise the VE is a slightly more carbonated and refreshing blend of the mixture as before.

VE RANGE

Now to Valiant's 1968 range. The VE line-up consists of three model series instead of the previous two: the plain bottom-of-line Valiant, medium-range Regal, and top-line VIP, which adds such goodies as a floor console gear selector, driver's headrest and super-lush upholstery.

Price structure is complicated, to say the least, because of the safety packages and the fact that the optional, more powerful engines are available on any model in the range — for the first time. Previously there was the 145 bhp six line and the V8 line, and the engines were not interchangeable between them. Now Chrysler follow Ford into the thousand-and-one options market.

Here's how it goes . . .

Prices start at $2490 for the manual Valiant with unchanged 145 bhp six. Regals start at $3095 with the same engine but better seats, and the like.

On either of these can be specified the six uprated to 160 bhp, plus 100 mph tyres, for $60 — or the V8 uprated to 195 bhp, with 100 mph tyres and front power disc brakes for $210 (except on Regals, where this option costs $240 because some fancy trim goes into the package). But you can't have the V8 on any model without automatic transmission, which costs another $240.

On top of this, other extras are power steering (on automatics only, because the manual column change linkage fouls up the fitting arrangements) for $140, disc brakes when not mandatory in a V8 package $45, and $10 for front lap safety belts.

At this point things get almost simple. The VIP comes only with V8 and automatic power steering, discs, and lap-and-sash safety belts. Price, $3650.

Safari station wagons are $200 extra on all saloons except the VIP, where the difference is only $70. Why is that? Perhaps it would be easier to get your friendly dealer to explain.

Tyre sizes as well as types have changed. All models use 6.95 x 14in. instead of the previous 6.45 x 14. The 100 mph tyres with the performance engines are nylon — except for the VIP, which has Goodyear D70 wide-tread 125 mph tyres as standard.

All cars and wagons have a common new body. Overall length is up 5.5in. to 193.7in. on the saloons, and by 3.52in. to 192.5in. on the wagons. Width of both is increased by 0.75in. to 69.7in., wheelbase by 2in. to 108in., front track by 1.5in. to 57.4in. Curved side glass increases back and front shoulder-room (depending where your shoulders are) by 2in. Back-seat leg-room is up 1.5in.

Chrysler have NOT gone for the hippy look of the XR Falcon and the coming HK Holden. The lines are a logical styling development from the previous model.

Many new features

Other changes worth noting:

All dashes are well-padded along the top, with control knobs properly recessed.

The bonnet catch is released from inside — on all models.

Manual-shift linkage has been changed to give shorter and lighter travel between gears.

Power steering is of the co-axial type and steering-wheel turns are cut from four-plus to 3.75.

Screen-wiper motor is more powerful — and mounted on the engine bulkhead, where it can be got at easily. Wiper switch incorporates the control for the screen-washers, which are now electric instead of pump-type.

Floor dipswitch has been moved out from under the clutch pedal, where it was dangerously awkward, to say the least.

Air deflectors to keep the back window clean are standard on all Safari models — and ALL models now have an outside rear-vision mirror as standard. Padded sun-visors on all models, too. Dull-finished wiper blades, again on all models.

Last — and it should be first — dual braking systems on all models, meaning that total brake loss is almost beyond possibility.

Main modifications to the six-cylinder engine to produce 160 bhp are a two-choke carburettor and revised camshaft. Maximum torque is 220 lb./ft. at 2500 rpm.

The 273 cu. in. V8 puts out 195 bhp at 4400 rpm, and maximum torque of 265 lb./ft. at 2000 rpm, with the help of better carburation and revised camshaft.

As the figures suggest, both engines are not only smooth but highly accelerative from low revs. They certainly work well within their capacity and should give the same service as in earlier form, provided the extra is not constantly used or abused.

Chrysler make great play about the safety-with-power aspect of the VE — Power-Safe they call it. How safe?

Can any car-maker claim to be really interested in safety if he does not provide front safety belts as standard equipment, whether his car is fast or slow? Statistics say that most accidents happen at less than 40 mph, less than 20 miles from home, and that safety belts are the greatest single device that can be fitted to protect occupants. One of the cheapest, too.

Can the fitting as original equipment on the 145 bhp base model of standard 85 mph tyres be justified? It will easily cruise at 90.

Can the far-les-than-perfect drum brakes allowed with the 145 bhp and 160 bhp engine options be considered adequate? The new base model is over 1.5 cwt. heavier than the previous one.

Can body styling that shrouds both head and tail lights from the sides of the car be tolerated any longer?

Full marks for the idea — but the execution could have been a lot more thorough.

Finally, while the new body looks stylish and handsome, it is not so impressive on the score of function — see my previous remarks on seating arrangements inside.

Still, Valiant is as Valiant does — and this one does very well indeed. •

"Is that why they're called the opposite sex?"

MODERN MOTOR road TEST

DATA SHEET— CHRYSLER VALIANT 6

Manufacturer: Chrysler Australia Ltd., Tonsley Park, Adelaide. Test car supplied by them.

Price as tested $2835.

SPECIFICATIONS

ENGINE

Water cooled, six cylinders in line, cast iron block, four main bearings.

Bore x stroke	3.40 x 4.125in.
Capacity	225 cu. in.
Compression	8.4 to 1
Carburettor	one twin-choke
Fuel pump	mechanical
Fuel tank	15.0 gallons
Fuel recommended	super
Valve gear	pushrod ohv
Max. power (gross)	160 bhp at 4500 rpm
Max. torque	220 lb./ft. at 2500 rpm
Electrical system	12v, 45 amp hr. battery, 35 amp alternator

TRANSMISSION

Torqueflite automatic, three-speed.

Gear	Ratio	Overall	Mph/1000 rpm	Max. mph
Rev.	2.20	7.11	6.00	—
1st	2.45	7.91	7.72	38
2nd	1.45	4.68	13.60	71
3rd	1.00	3.23	22.80	98.8
Final drive ratio				3.23 to 1

CHASSIS

Wheelbase	9ft 0in.
Track front	4ft. 9.4in.
Track rear	4ft. 7.6in.
Length	16ft. 1.7in.
Width	5ft. 9.7in.
Height	4ft. 7in.
Clearance	7.2in.
Test weight	29.8 cwt.
Weight distribution front/rear	54/46%
lb./bhp	lb.

SUSPENSION

Front: Independent by lateral, non-parallel controls arms and torsion bars, telescopic hydraulic shock absorbers.

Back: Live axle with semi-elliptic leaf springs, telescopic hydraulic shock absorbers.

Brakes: disc/drum, servo assisted; 254.5 sq. in. of swept area.

Steering	Worm and ball nut
Turns lock to lock	4.4
Turning circle	37.5ft.

Wheels: Steel disc with 6.95 by 14 tubeless cross ply tyres.

PERFORMANCE

Top speed	100.4 mph
Average (both ways)	98.8 mph
Standing quarter mile	18.9 sec.

Acceleration in D range using full kick-down

Zero to	seconds
30 mph	3.8
40 mph	5.8
50 mph	7.6
60 mph	12.6
70 mph	18.8
80 mph	27.1
20-40 mph	4.0
30-50 mph	4.9
40-60 mph	7.2
50-70 mph	9.8
60-80 mph	10.9

Consumption: 18.7 mpg over 111 miles, including all tests.

Speedo error:

Indicated mph	30	40	50	60	70	80
Actual mph	30	40	49	58	68	78

ACCELERATION CHART

drive

ss ¼

inter.

low

12 D N R P

MPH

TIME IN SECONDS ▶

HOW CHRYSLER VALIANT COMPARES

60	70	80	90	100
Chrysler Valiant VE ($2835)				
Chrysler Valiant VC ($2730)				
Holden 186 ($2566)				
Falcon 200 ($2661)				

MAXIMUM SPEED (mean) M.P.H.

25	15	5
Chrysler Valiant VE		
Chrysler Valiant VC		
Holden 186		
Falcon 200		

0-60 M.P.H. SECONDS

40	30	20
Chrysler Valiant VE		
Chrysler Valiant VC		
Holden 186		
Falcon 200		

M.P.G. Overall

30	20	10
Chrysler Valiant VE		
Chrysler Valiant VC		
Holden 186		
Falcon 200		

STANDING-START ¼-MILE (secs.)

Valiant V.I.P.

LUXURIOUS 195 H.P. V8 WITH DISC BRAKES AND POWER STEERING

The special car for Very Important People

Highlights of Valiant VIP

NEW LUXURY: Individual, comfort contoured seats for driver and front passenger. Both front seats are fully reclining and have adjustable head-rests for added comfort and safety. Rear seat has a folding centre arm-rest. Upholstery is in luxury sponge vinyl; Floors fully carpeted; Doors trimmed to full height and have a subtle touch of distinction with a wood grained panel feature. Equipment is practical and complete:— New, quiet in operation Heater/Demister; Power-operated windscreen washers with control from instrument panel; Shatterproof Prismatic interior rear view mirror; Exterior rear view mirror standard; Ashtrays in rear door armrests; Wheel-trim rings; Courtesy lights all doors; Big luggage boot carpeted and with trunk light; Reversing lights standard.

DISTINCTIVE NEW LOOK OF LEADERSHIP: Valiant's elegant, long look is enhanced in the V.I.P. by a vinyl covered roof and distinctive body mouldings. The use of gently curved side glass adds extra seating width inside, but still keeps a sleek look outside. New, big concave rear window and bigger side windows add to all-round visibility. New design wind-screen pillar gives easier entry to front compartment. With a 2″ increase in wheelbase (now 108″) and 5.5″ in overall length (193.7″), the car not only looks more impressive, but also provides additional rear seat leg room.

"POWER-SAFE" DRIVING: The Valiant V8 engine now develops 195 HP. The dynamic performance is safety-matched with power-assisted, front disc brakes; Dual braking system with warning light; Power steering; 125 mph nylon cord tyres; An even wider front track (increased 1.5″ to 57.4″); Torsion bar suspension; Safety interiors. Detailed refinements have been made to the suspension to provide an even smoother, softer ride. For added convenience, an underhood engine lamp is provided.

3-SPEED TORQUEFLITE AND POWER STEERING: In the V.I.P. sedan, gear selection is made through a short, sports-type lever mounted in a fully trimmed floor console. Co-axial power steering provides finger-tip parking and effortless steering control.

BRIEF SPECIFICATIONS

DIMENSIONS: Wheelbase 108″; Overall length 193.7″ (Sedan), 192.5″ (Safari); Overall width 69.7″ ... Overall height 55″.
ENGINE: V8, O.H.V.; Capacity 273 cu. in.; Bore 3.63″; Stroke 3.31″; Comp. ratio 8.8:1; Max. BHP @ r.p.m. 195 @ 4400; Max. Torque @ r.p.m. 265 lbs./ft. @ 2000.
BRAKES: Power assisted, front disc brakes, Duo-servo, self adjusting hydraulic rear. Dual braking system.
SUSPENSION: Front . . Independent, lateral, non-parallel control arms with torsion bars. Rear . . . Longitudinal leaf springs.
TRANSMISSION: Torqueflite 3-speed automatic.
WHEELS AND TYRES: D70 x 14 x 4, 125 mph nylon cord; Double-sided Safety-rim wheels.

SAFARI V.I.P. (illustrated bottom right): Has the same mechanical speci-fications as the sedan but for maximum passenger room has gearshift selector on steering column. Tailgate is power-operated and with internal and external controls. Roof rack standard. Rear compartment floor carpeted. Rear compartment dome light. Front seat includes centre armrest.

CHRYSLER AUSTRALIA LTD.

Valiant .. Built to lead... Built to last!

5/10001020

VF SERIES (1969)

ABOVE (and PREVIOUS PAGE): The VF Pacer.

27 March 1969 brought the announcement of the VF Valiant series — a range of facelifted VEs which would have been unremarkable but for the introduction of a high-performance model called Pacer.

The Pacer four-door sports sedan was variously described as 'the surprise of the year' and 'Chrysler's most original creation'.

People were surprised because the Pacer was chasing the young high-performance motorist. Until then, this type of buyer had been ignored by Chrysler and, in turn, had ignored (or been unable to afford) virtually anything with a Valiant badge.

The other new variant in the VF range was the luxury Regal 770, marketed to replace the old VIP (which was soon to be replaced by a new bigger VIP).

At the time the VF series was released, Valiant's sales were good but its overall market share was marginally falling. Chrysler began firing all guns to win it back.

The VF range also brought a bigger version of the V-8 engine (the 'Fireball 318'), a wider range of seating, more safety features (in anticipation of government legislation) and increased soundproofing. Factory-installed integrated air-conditioning became an option

on all models and the Chrysler system proved to be just about the best on offer.

Distinguished from the previous model by new grille, headlights and tail-lights, the VF had the front parking lights and turn signal lights recessed into the top of the guards. This was popular as a styling feature but did not make for very clear signals on sunny days.

The VF also had unusual repeater lights on the rear of the sedan. The grille was a horizontal bar affair.

The Pacer was identified by a black and red grille treatment, red paint-filled boot lid moulding, 'sports type' (i.e. fake mag) wheel covers, narrow waist-high body striping and Pacer 225 insignia.

It was powered by a high-compression version of the 3.69-litre 'Slant Six' engine (9.2:1 versus 8.4:1), which had been developed at Chrysler's Lonsdale plant. Equipped with a two-barrel carburettor, this engine developed around 130 kW (175 bhp) while producing much more torque than the standard version. Interestingly, Chrysler never released an official power output figure for the Pacer.

The Pacer had a Borg Warner three-speed floor-shift gearbox. This, the first manual floor shift since that of the original R Series, had an

'H' layout with reverse gear directly above first and no lock-out. This unusual arrangement prompted some embarrassing incidents when potential buyers test-drove the Pacer. When starting from traffic lights, they had a marked tendency to restyle cars parked behind.

More favourable Pacer features included finned drum brakes front and rear (power-boosted front discs were optional), a front anti-roll bar and a low-restriction exhaust system. The suspension was lowered by half an inch (the car was still using the Valiant's rather dated but adequate torsion bar system).

High-back reclining seats were fitted. Described variously as 'aircraft-style seats' and 'tombstones', these represented the first serious attempt at whiplash-preventing head-restraints seen on an Australian car. The Pacer's instrument dials were white with black lettering and included a tachometer mounted on top of the panel.

Handling was much improved and the car had the speed to match its name. *Modern Motor* writers boasted they had achieved a 17.5-second quarter mile and reached 173 km/h (108 mph) by the end of their test strip. And that was in a car with just 300 km on the clock!

Strange as it sounds, a Pacer wagon was considered. Two pre-production cars were built before the idea was shelved.

The Regal 770 had a typical Regal equipment level and the new Fireball 318 engine developing 172 kW (230 bhp). There was no wagon variant.

Added to the newcomers were facelifted versions of the VE Valiant and Regal. A wide choice of metallic finishes was offered across the range, except on the Pacer which had special 'individual' colour schemes. It came in just three colours: Wild Red, Wild Blue and Wild Yellow.

The carryover models (Valiant and Regal)

The Regal 770.

The Regal interior.

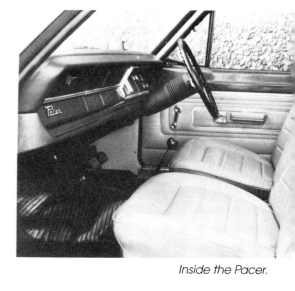

Inside the Pacer.

were largely unchanged mechanically but incorporated some worthwhile safety additions including an instrument panel with extra padding and an energy-absorbing steering column. GM-H had already released a telescopic steering column but Valiant's was superior as it would not only telescope but also collapse from either side in a collision.

The Regal V-8 wagon received a power-operated tailgate window.

The 'Sure-Grip' limited-slip differential was offered as an option across the new range with a choice of rear axle ratios. The standard axle ratio for six-cylinder VF Valiants was 3.23:1 and, for eight-cylinder vehicles, it was 2.92:1. The latter was optional for six-cylinder units with Sure-Grip and a third ratio (3.5:1) was also available.

The VF price range started at $2598 for the base-model manual sedan and reached $3628 for the Regal 770 sedan.

The Pacer, available only in manual form, cost $2798.

In May 1969 came the new VIP. This time, however, the VIP was given a separate identity from the Valiant, echoing the way Fairlane had always been marketed as a 'Ford', not a 'Falcon'.

The announcement accompanying the release of the VIP said: 'Chrysler Australia Ltd is to enter the luxury segment of larger popular vehicles with a long wheelbase car intermediate between its Valiant range and Dodge Phoenix. The new car will be marketed as "VIP By Chrysler".'

For the first time, the local company was making a car bigger than the Valiant. It was an answer to the Fairlane and Holden's curious Brougham, which had a standard wheelbase and a massive boot to increase its length.

The VIP had a wheelbase of 2850 mm (112 inches) — 100 mm longer than the Valiant. Although very Valiant-like, it was slightly different in styling with dual headlights, a different rear light treatment and what was advertised as a 'limousine' rear window. The vinyl roof was thickly padded and came in black, green or parchment. No VIP station wagon was offered.

The VIP engine choice was between the 120 kW (160 bhp) 'Slant Six' and the 172 kW (230 bhp) Fireball 318 5.2-litre (318 cubic inches) V-8. Automatic transmission was standard with both engines.

Equipment levels were high with full carpeting, armrests on all doors and in the centre of the front and rear seats, heater-demister, dual horns, lights in the engine compartment and boot, courtesy switches and pockets on all doors, a vanity mirror mounted inside the glovebox lid, a soft-grip steering wheel, distinctive wheel trims and a fake wood-grain finish on the instrument panel and door trim.

Whitewall tyres were fitted to the VIP — 6.95 section on the Six and 7.35 section on the V-8.

As Ford had done with the Fairlane, Chrysler offered a 'de-specced' variant of the VIP. This had the six-cylinder 120 kW (160 bhp) engine and a front bench seat.

ABOVE: The Chrysler VIP.
BELOW: The workhorses — Valiant Safari wagon and Wayfarer utility.

Coaxial power steering and front disc brakes were standard equipment on the V-8 VIP and optional on the Six. The V-8 had the transmission selector lever mounted in a floor console. Integrated air-conditioning was available as a factory option.

Safety features included the Valiant's new energy-absorbing steering column plus a padded steering wheel cover. Base price of the VIP was $3598 for the Six or from $3998 for the V-8.

There was also action in the coupe-front. Determined to join Holden's Monaro in the new coupe-market, Chrysler released its own two-door.

The VF Valiant Hardtop was announced on 12 September 1969 in a range of six models and with a choice between a six-cylinder and a V-8 engine.

Contrary to the popular assumption (fuelled by the Pacer) that the newcomer would fight Monaro and Falcon GT on their own terms, the Hardtop turned out to be a luxury-orientated vehicle with a restrained appearance.

Its length was nothing short of enormous. With a 2820 mm (111 inches) wheelbase — just short of the VIP length — it had a massive tail which took the overall length to just over 5000 mm (200 inches) — 100 mm longer than the VIP. The Hardtop was easily the longest coupe ever built in Australia. The door openings were a vast 1070 mm in width.

The Hardtop models were named after the sedans, i.e. Valiant, Regal and Regal 770, and carried similar trim, mechanical specifications and front-end sheet metal.

This use of sedan sheet metal was to maintain the local content as much as possible while avoiding huge retooling costs. All other Hardtop body panels were imported.

A range of 'two-tone' roofs and vinyl roofs was offered and the Fireball 318 V-8 was an option for all Hardtop models.

Despite its size, the Hardtop handled surprisingly well, albeit with the usual dash of Chrysler understeer. It wasn't, however, fun to reverse a Hardtop into a tight car-parking space.

Hardtop prices started at $2898, rising to $3838 for the Regal 770.

There were 52 944 VF Valiants made. The enormous model proliferation seen in the late 1960s had been good for picking up extra sales but the cost of offering such a large range was becoming too high.

In many ways the end of the 1960s signalled the beginning of the end of Valiant's success story. But there were many interesting and successful models to follow.

The new Hardtop: The Regal 770 (ABOVE and BELOW) and Regal (BELOW LEFT).

DATA SHEET— VALIANT REGAL

Manufacturer: Chrysler (Aust.) Pty. Ltd.
Test car supplied by them.
Price as tested: $3969.

SPECIFICATIONS

ENGINE

Water cooled, six cylinders in line; cast iron block, four main bearings.

Bore x stroke	3.4 x 4.125in.
Capacity	3697 cc.; 225 cu. in.
Compression	8.4 to 1
Carburettor	2 bbl downdraught
Fuel pump	mechanical
Fuel tank	15 gallons
Fuel recommended	super
Valve gear	pushrod ohv
Max. power (gross)	160 bhp at 4500 rpm
Max. torque	220 lb. ft. at 2500 rpm
Electrical system	12v, 45 amp hr. battery, 35 amp alternator

TRANSMISSION

Three-speed torque converter automatic.

Gear	Ratio	Overall	Max. mph
Reverse	2.20	7.11	—
Low	2.45	7.91	39
Intermediate	1.45	4.68	70
Drive	1.00	3.23	98
Final drive ratio			3.23 to 1

CHASSIS

Wheelbase	9ft. 0in.
Track front	4ft. 9½in.
Track rear	4ft. 7½in.
Length	16ft. 1¾in.
Width	5ft. 9¾in.
Height	4ft. 7in.
Clearance	7¼in.
Test weight	1 ton 9 cwt. 90 lb.
Weight distribution front/rear	54/46%

SUSPENSION

Front: Independent by lateral, non-parallel control arms and torsion bars, telescopic hydraulic shock absorbers.
Rear: Live axle with semi-elliptic leaf springs, telescopic hydraulic shock absorbers.

Brakes: 9in. drum, 254 sq. in. of swept area.

Steering	worm and ball nut
Turns lock to lock	4.4
Turning circle	37.5ft.

Wheels: Steel disc with 6.95 by 14 tubeless cross ply tyres.

PERFORMANCE

Top speed	98.8 mph
Average (both ways)	97.6 mph
Standing quarter-mile	19.1 sec.

Acceleration

Zero to	sec.
30 mph	4.2
40 mph	6.3
50 mph	9.7
60 mph	13.7
70 mph	18.7
80 mph	26.5

	full kickdown
20-40 mph	5.2
30-50 mph	6.2
40-60 mph	7.0
50-70 mph	9.2

BRAKING: Five crash stops from 60 mph.

Stop	percent G	pedal pressure
1	.78	72 lb.
2	.74	76 lb.
3	.70	76 lb.
4	.68	80 lb.
5	.64	85 lb.

Consumption: 15.1 mpg over 318 miles, including all tests; 18 mpg in normal country and suburban use.

Speedo error: Accurate throughout range.

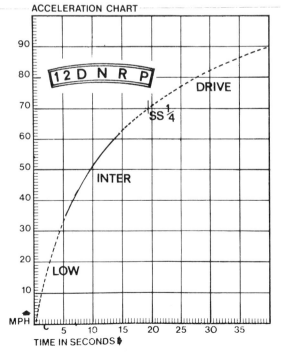

ACCELERATION CHART

1 2 D N R P

DRIVE

SS ¼

INTER

LOW

MPH

TIME IN SECONDS

HOW VALIANT REGAL COMPARES

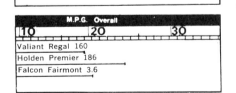

MAXIMUM SPEED (mean) M.P.H.

60 70 80 90 100

Valiant Regal 160 ($3969)
Holden Premier 186 ($3070)
Falcon Fairmont 3.6 ($3283)

0-60 M.P.H. SECONDS

25 15 5

Valiant Regal 160
Holden Premier 186
Falcon Fairmont 3.6

M.P.G. Overall

10 20 30

Valiant Regal 160
Holden Premier 186
Falcon Fairmont 3.6

STANDING-START ¼-MILE (secs.)

30 20 10

Valiant Regal 160
Holden Premier 186
Falcon Fairmont 3.6

VG SERIES (1970)

Stirling Moss and 'friend'.

But for the rectangular headlights and a few other minor exterior changes, one could be excused for thinking that Chrysler Australia was seeing in the 1970s exactly the same way it had seen out the sixties.

The new VG series carried on basically the same sedan, Hardtop and Safari wagon body styles. Interior changes were minimal and there were no claims about an improved ride or handling.

But Chrysler officials had something to shout about — and they practically screamed. Their big weapon was the completely new Australian-made 4-litre 'Hemi 245' engine.

The new engine was released with a bold anouncement:

'After five years' development work by a team of engineers at Lonsdale (SA), Chrysler Australia

has introduced a completely new six-cylinder engine to give its 1970 Valiant range a power and fuel economy advantage over all other six-cylinder engined cars produced in Australia.

'Chrysler believes the new engine, named the Hemi 245, to be the most advanced six-cylinder power plant made anywhere in the world.'

Three versions of the engine were offered. A 123 kW (165 bhp) Hemi was fitted to the base Valiant and a 138 kW (185 bhp) 'two-barrel' (dual-throat carburettor) unit with a modified camshaft came with the VIP, Regal 770 sedan and Hardtop.

A 'high-performance' version of the two-barrel engine was made solely for the Valiant Pacer sports sedan. For some reason, Chrysler continued to be cagey about releasing the output figure for the Pacer but it was in the range of 142-146 kW (190-195 bhp).

Chrysler Australia spent around $33 million on the Hemi and went to enormous lengths to promote this 'major advance in Australian automotive engineering'. Among other things, the company brought retired British racing driver Stirling Moss to Australia to explain the 'Hemi' concept to potential buyers in a series of lavish advertisements.

Apart from the hydraulic valve lifter, the Hemi was completely built in Australia. It showed that Chrysler had judged the 'big six' to be the type of power plant Australians would prefer in the years ahead. Holden had recently addressed the same question and opted for the V-8, producing its 4.2-litre '253' with an investment of over $22 million.

The Hemi began its life in early 1966 on the drafting boards of the US Chrysler Corporation's design department. It was called the 'D' engine and was intended to be used in a range of medium-sized trucks.

Work on the Australian engine commenced within a few months of the US project. At first a single-cylinder development unit was built and the configuration was sorted out. A single-overhead camshaft and even a V-6 layout were considered for the Australian Valiant before the adoption of the overhead valve 'straight six' design was finalised.

Prototype engines were made in the US and these were immediately followed by some made at Lonsdale. Much of the detail design of the engine was finalised in Australia. Chrysler Australia set up a new Engine Design and Development Department in early 1967 and completely took over the engine's development.

A few VF Valiants (designated 'VFX') were fitted with the Australian Hemi 245 engine to fully evaluate it before its sales release in the VG model. The Hemi engine was of oversquare design with hydraulic tappets and a seven-bearing cast-iron crankshaft. It introduced many new and advanced features in Australian manufacture and was clearly the best Australian Six of the day.

The name 'Hemi' was derived from the engine's hemispherical combustion chambers. Chrysler claimed the hemispherical head allowed the use of larger intake and exhaust valves to bring about an improved flow of the fuel-air mixture and the exhaust gases. It also enabled the valves to be placed in better positions to facilitate the swirl of gases inside the combustion chambers.

A major advantage was that the new engine was 16 per cent more powerful and 18 kg (40 lbs) lighter than the stalwart 'Slant Six', which hadn't significantly changed in nearly a decade of use in Valiants.

The Hemi engaged in police work.

Each of the three Hemi engines had its own colour scheme. The 245 single-barrel had a red block, silver rocker cover and air cleaner, and a white fan; the 245 two-barrel had a red block, 'black crackle' rocker cover and air cleaner, and a white fan; and the Pacer engine an orange-red block, yellow rocker cover and air cleaner, and a white fan. Each carried a decal bearing the words 'Made solely in Australia — by Chrysler'.

The Hemi received a good reception from the press, which praised its power and very even torque curve but suggested it was fairly noisy and not particularly smooth.

With the aim of increasing the local content, Chrysler was in the process of quietly phasing out the smooth and quiet US-built TorqueFlite automatic transmission in favour of Borg Warner's locally built, three-speed torque convertor automatic. This gearbox was less smooth than the acclaimed TorqueFlite but the ratios were arguably better matched to the new engine.

The VG range offered a wide (and complicated) range of power train combinations, based on manual and automatic transmissions, three types of Hemi 245 engine, the 318 V-8 and the 225 engine which had powered previous models (the 225 version was built mainly for export).

By now the V-8 was an option available only with the Regal Safari, Regal 770 and VIP models.

The Pacer 245 still had the three-speed manual gearbox, the Regal 770 sedan and Hardtop had automatic as standard, all other

models were available in manual and/or automatic depending on the selected engine.

Body-wise, the VG was a further development of the same theme. To give the cars a fresh look, the new models had rectangular (rather than round) headlights, restyled rear lights and each variant had a distinctive grille, set of badges and other identifying features.

The base Valiant had new black mouldings running the full length of the body sides. Larger 'Valiant' emblem hubcaps were used throughout the range and front fender badges denoted each model's Hemi 245 engine category. This designation was also featured on the rear of the cars.

The Regal featured new wheel arch mouldings, larger hubcaps with Regal emblems and a full-width feature panel on the rear deck.

New trim materials were offered and a new-look instrument panel featured an 'open face' instrument cluster design. Each model had a different cluster face, with the Regal having a fake wood-grain surround. Both the Pacer and the Regal 770 were equipped with a tachometer.

The Pacer had new, lower seats and front and rear carpet replacing the former model's rubber floor mats. An optional 'Mod Pack' included black bonnet patches and 'spoiler stripes' for the sides and across the boot.

With the VG, Chrysler introduced a new ventilated disc brake with a floating head caliper which gave improved performance with reduced pedal effort. This allowed the introduction of disc brakes without power assistance in some models, because the pedal effort in the non-boosted form was the same as that for the drum brakes in previous models. These unboosted front discs were fitted as standard to the Pacer, the two-barrel six-cylinder Regal and all VIP models.

Chrysler Australia was still pushing its VIP as a separate identity and finding the same problem that General Motors-Holden's was to have with its Statesman — people still called it by the same name as the model from which it was derived, i.e. Valiant VIP and Holden Statesman.

The 1970 VIP became the first Australian-made car to be fitted with air-conditioning as standard. It also had an electric clock. The VIP came with the 138 kW (185 bhp) Hemi 245 or with the 172 kW (230 bhp) V-8 as an option. Interestingly, those who ordered the V-8 got a 13-transistor push-button radio as standard.

The base '245' VG Valiant sedan sold for $2686, the automatic Regal was $3483 in six-cylinder form, the 770 V-8 was $3748. The top-of-the-line VIP automatic with V-8 was $4332. The Pacer cost $3229.

At about this time Chrysler claimed that 60 per cent of its sales was made up of Regal models.

In early August Chrysler combined two popular models and came up with the two-door Pacer Hardtop. Longer than the sedan by 190 mm (7 inches), the Pacer Hardtop was fitted with the same high-performance Hemi 245 as the standard Pacer. It retained most features of the sedan including the grille and optional 'Mod Pack'.

One of the few modifications made was that the bucket seats were positioned lower. As with all Valiant Hardtops, the two-door Pacer was short on rear passenger room.

The Pacer Hardtop price was $3178.

Showing all its 'mod' flair, Chrysler offered the new model in Bondi Bleach White, Thar She Blue, Little Hood Riding Red, Hot Mustard and Hemi Orange. Trim colours were a little more restrained: red, neutral and black.

The new release saw Chrysler maintain its lead in the performance-for-dollars market —

little could touch the Pacer sedan or Hardtop for straight-line performance.

One interesting 'hot' Valiant which never made the showroom floor was a 340 V-8 VG sedan fitted with a four-speed (Hurst shift) manual transmission from the US. Chrysler Australia built a prototype — which proved to be extraordinarily quick — but the project went no further.

Chrysler advertised that the 1970 Valiant had 96 per cent Australian component content.

In early 1971 manufacture of the 'Slant Six' engine — which had been introduced with the R Series in 1962 and was still being fitted to export models — finally stopped. A 3.53-litre '215' Hemi took its place and this was also sold on the Australian market.

Unfortunately, there had been massive discounting of VF Valiants just before the release of the VG. This led to buyer resistance to paying full price for the VG which, after all, looked very similar. So despite the Hemi engine, initial VG sales were disappointing.

There were 46 374 VG Valiants made.

VG Hardtop (ABOVE) and Pacer Hardtop (BELOW).

"VALIANT
THE RIGHT CARS FOR ALL
THE RIGHT REASONS."

STIRLING MOSS

ABOVE and OVERLEAF: 1970 Chrysler brochure.

HEMI PACER
The clean machine for all the right reasons.
Clean, no-nonsense styling and pure performance are what
Hemi Pacer is all about. The toughest 6 cylinder
engine we make is standard: The Hi-Performance
245 2-barrel carburettor Hemi. It moves quicker with the
"Track Pack" option. Styling is out of sight and can
be made wilder with an optional "Mod Pack".
Aircraft-type bucket seats, three-on-the-floor, big
11" discs up front, the Pacer's got it all.
If the quarter-mile is your thing, drop in an optional
Sure Grip 3.23:1 differential. You've got to test-drive
this machine to believe it. Do it. For all the right reasons.

REGAL 770 2-DOOR HARDTOP
The right move for all the right reasons.
This is the car that people will move up to in 1970.
Clean lines and sporty styling.
Big 111" wheelbase for a smooth comfortable ride.
Reclining, buffalo-grain vinyl bucket seats, with head rests
are standard. So is the smart centre console and
Torqueflite automatic transmission.
Options include everything from a remote outside rear-view
mirror, to integrated air conditioning with tinted glass.
The 2-door Hardtop comes in three models.
Regal 770, Regal and Valiant. Each one is a
move up. For all the right reasons.

VALIANT PACER 245

MODERN MOTOR road TEST

Detail refinements, "go faster" tape, and — most important of all — a more muscular engine with hemispherical combustion chambers, make the Pacer a better car

THANKS to a sustained and interesting advertising campaign, we all now know pretty well ~~th~~at a hemi is.

~~W~~hat we've been endeavouring to do ~~in~~ the last few days is to find out how ~~the~~ hemi goes. The answer, in as few ~~wo~~rds as possible is — pretty well.

~~T~~he object of this test — the hemi ~~24~~5 Pacer — probably sells in less ~~nu~~mbers than any other car in ~~Ch~~rysler's new range (with the possible ~~ex~~ception of the VIP), but it is safe to ~~sa~~y that it commands the most interest ~~am~~ong both Valiant owners and ~~wo~~uld-be owners, and just motorists ~~ge~~nerally.

~~I~~n some strange way the Pacer has ~~ca~~ptured the public imagination. The ~~ne~~w model can only improve on the ~~car~~'s already favourable image.

~~T~~he best part about the Pacer is of ~~co~~urse that new engine — an engine ~~who~~se precise output remains hidden ~~be~~hind a veil of Chrysler hooha. It's ~~ab~~out 190-195 bhp — not bad ~~co~~nsidering that a few years ago the ~~thre~~e-litre V8s were giving about this, ~~an~~d aren't giving much more right ~~no~~w.

~~W~~e plan to publish a detailed ~~te~~chnical run-down in a ~~no~~t-too-distant issue, but for now here ~~ar~~e a few facts on the motor.

~~F~~or a start, it has a cubic capacity of ~~24~~5 cu. in. — 20 more "cubes" than the slant six that powered last year's Pacer.

It is oversquare, measuring 3.76 in. across the bore, and 3.68 in. in the stroke

Compression ratio is 9.5 to 1, and a double-choke downdraught carburettor is used.

Valve actuation is by means of hydraulic tappets, and down below the crankshaft runs in seven main bearings to ensure durability and improve smoothness.

A split exhaust manifold and high lift camshaft complete the Pacer picture.

The motor is coupled, via a diaphragm spring clutch to a new three-speed manual transmission, with a floor shift arrangement.

The shift is stiffish, and has the disadvantage of not having a lock-out on reverse, which is in the position occupied by first on a normal four-speed shift.

Limited slip differential was fitted to the test car, and this helped considerably getting that generous power to the ground.

Speaking of acceleration, consider if you will the improvement wrought by the new engine. We thought the slant-six Pacer was a pretty honest performer, but the new car puts it to shame. We managed a standing quarter in 16.4 sec. whereas the best recorded in the earlier car was 17.9.

Improvements

We're inclined to think that the car would be further improved by the fitting of wider wheels — 5½in. rims are standard, and the test car was fitted with Olympic radial ply tyres. We can think of no reason why 6 in. rims should not make a significant improvement to adhesion, and subsequently, pointability.

Overall gearing is fairly tall, thanks to a final drive ratio of 3.23 to 1. Maximums in gears are 42, 76, and 114 mph, although in the indirect ratios we found it more conducive to rapid acceleration to change gears a few mph before these maxima.

Suspension is good old Valiant torsion bars, non-parallel control arms, anti-sway bar and tele shock absorbers at front, and a rigid axle with semi ellipties and tele shock absorbers at the rear. On most surfaces this set-up works very smoothly, and is generally less hysterical in its behaviour on very rough surfaces than the GM-H and Ford competition.

But a combination of power on, and rough surfaces can send the Pacer sideways very rapidly, and when this happens the pilot has his hands very fully of not-very-fast steering.

The same sort of thing happens on slick bitumen too, and the unwary young driver who takes his brand new Pacer out in the rain should be extremely careful.

MODERN MOTOR road TEST

DATA SHEET— PACER 245

Manufacturer: Chrysler Aust. Pty. Ltd., Adelaide, S.A.
Test car supplied by them.
Price as tested: $2978

ENGINE

Water cooled, 6 cylinders in line. Cast iron block, seven main bearings.
Bore x stroke: .... 3.76 x 3.68 in.
Capacity .... 245 cu. in.
Compression .... 9.5 to 1.
Carburettor .... 2 bbl d'draught
Fuel pump .... mechanical
Fuel tank .... 16 gallons
Fuel recommended .... super
Valve gear .... p'rod ohv
Max. power (gross) .... NA
Max. torque .... NA
Electrical system .. 12v, 45 amp hr battery,
                           35 amp alternator

TRANSMISSION

Three speed manual all synchro gearbox. Single dry plate clutch.

Gear	Ratio	Max. mph.
Rev.	3.67	—
1st.	2.71	42
2nd.	1.55·	76
3rd.	1.00	114

Final drive ratio .... 3.23 to 1

CHASSIS

Wheelbase .... 9ft. 0in.
Track front .... 4ft. 10½in.

Track rear .... 4ft. 8½in.
Length .... 16ft. 4in.
Width .... 5ft. 9¾in.
Clearance .... 6in.
Kerb weight .... 1 ton 6cwt. 0lbs.

SUSPENSION

Front: Independent by torsion bars, non-parallel control arms, anti-sway bar, telescopic shock absorbers.
Rear: Live axle by semi-elliptic leaf springs, telescopic shock absorbers.
Brakes: 11in. dis/drum 482 sq. in. of swept area.
Steering: .... worm and ball
Turns lock to lock 4.4
Turning circle .... ft.
Wheels: Steel disc with 185 by 14 tubeless radial ply Olympic tyres.

PERFORMANCE

Top speed .... 116.8 mph
Average (both ways) .... 114.2 mph
Standing quarter mile .... 16.4 sec.
Acceleration
Zero to   seconds
30 mph 3.0
40 mph 4.3
50 mph 6.5
60 mph 8.8
70 mph 12.3
80 mph 17.2

		2nd	top
20 — 40 mph		3.8	5.4
30 — 50		3.9	5.7
40 — 60		3.8	6.4
50 — 70		4.8	6.9

BRAKING: Five crash stops from 60 mph

Stop	percent g	pedal pressure
1	.58	60 lb.
2	.74	60
3	.76	62
4	.72	64
5	.68	68

Consumption: 19 mpg over 386 miles including all tests: 22 — 23 mpg in normal country and suburban use.
Speedo error

Indicated mph	30 40 50 60 70 80
Actual mph	29 39 49 59 68 77

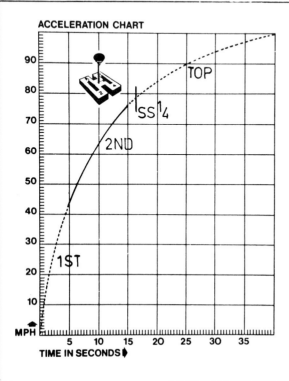

ACCELERATION CHART

TOP
SS¼
2ND
1ST

MPH
TIME IN SECONDS

HOW PACER 245 COMPARES

MAXIMUM SPEED (mean) M.P.H.

70 80 90 100 110 120 130

Valiant Pacer 225 ($2943)
Valiant Pacer 245 ($2978)
Holden Monaro 253 ($3443)

0-60 M.P.H. SECONDS

25 20 15 10 5

Valiant Pacer 225
Valiant Pacer 245
Holden Monaro 253

M.P.G. Overall

10 20 30 40

Valiant Pacer 225
Valiant Pacer 245
Holden Monaro 253

STANDING START ¼ MILE (secs)

20 10

Valiant Pacer 225
Valiant Pacer 245
Holden Monaro 253

VALIANT PACER 245

Of course, high quality rubber of the Michelin XAS or VR type would help. We drove the Pacers Chrysler was using in its abortive record attempts at Sandown in April and these were running on Michelin's pricey VR tyres. Despite very wet conditions, the cars felt very safe on the streaming track). The torsion bar suspension provides a nice level ride and the Pacer corners with not much body roll.

Handling characteristics are anything but neutral however. We found that the car was very willing to oversteer and for some reason this was more pronounced in right handers than left handers. It was however, reasonably controllable, and responded well to applications of lock and the less subtle method of simply backing off the throttle.

Braking was adequate. The Valiant range has swung to ventilated Kelsey-Hayes disc brakes — same as Ford — and these, fitted as standard to the Pacer work extremely well. Unlike other front disc/rear drum braking systems, the Pacer's is not servo-assisted.

Despite this, pedal effort is not excessive.

On our crash stop test, the first stop — the critical one in most emergency situations — was the least satisfactory. The rear drums locked up, and the car travelled further than it should have.

Fortunately, it didn't show any inclination to deviate off the straight-ahead.

Subsequent stops were achieved with no rear brake locking, and the best stop — the third — was .76g with 62 lb. of pedal.

The clutch pedal required a pressure of 35 lb. — not excessive by performance-car standards, but disconcerting in that the return spring action was strong and the result — initially at least — was bouncy take-offs.

The engine feels as if it could well be a winner. Interesting that Chrysler should pin its hopes in a big straight six, whereas GM-H has taken the opposite tack with a small V8.

The 245 Hemi starts easily, idles smoothly, and responds very promptly to the throttle. In the last respect it is quite outstanding.

But it is not as smooth an engine as we expected, nor as torquey low-down as we would have liked.

The Pacer will pull away from 20-or-so mph in top gear, but it isn't lively and there is a pronounced period of vibration before speed builds up.

Higher up the scale it is rough too. The tachometer is redlined at 5000 rpm, but we found the engine not-too-happy to go this high, and changed gears at about 4500 rpm, which corresponds to about 37 and 70 mph in the indirect ratios.

Chrysler's claims about their hemispherical combustion chambers improving economy seem to be well-founded. We averaged 21 mpg in commuting-type motoring, whereas the slant six Pacer tested about 12 months ago couldn't better 18.5 mpg. That's quite a worthwhile improvement.

Appointments

The Pacer is deliberately pared down to keep its price within the reach of young people interested in sporty type motor cars. Consequently the interior looks a little stark compared to other cars in the Chrysler range.

But that's to be expected in a car offering so many other things and costing only $2978.

Continued

VALIANT PACER

Continued

For all Chrysler's claims, the interior of the car still isn't as good as it could be. Sure, the instrumentation is a big improvement, but they persist in mounting the dipper button right under the brake pedal, and the screen washer button where the dipper should be.

The seats are quite good however. The back-rests don't have nearly as pronounced a headrest extension as the previous car, with the result that rearward visibility is improved.

The new instrument cluster had a unique distinction. It was the first Chrysler speedo we've calibrated in several tests that was inaccurate. Usually they're spot on. This one however, was a shade off.

Instrumentation generally is good. The dials are clearly calibrated — white on black with bright red needles that are easy to see.

Corded carpet is now fitted to the car, whereas the first Pacer had rubber mats. The carpet is an improvement, and together with the efficient heater/demister manages to make the cab quite cosy on cold nights.

Styling? The VG is substantially the same as the VF i.e., pretty old hat. But we're told that next year is new body year for the Valiant.

At least by keeping a body style for a number of years, Chrysler are able to get their body quality sorted out.

Panel fit and finish wasn't very good when the current shape was first introduced as the VE. But no such criticisms could be levelled at the VG Pacer.

But the car is certainly in need of a face lift. Maybe then the packaging will be as good as the lusty 245 Hemi hidden within. ●

MODERN MOTOR — JULY 1970

Another angle of the 'VG' VIP.

VH SERIES (1971)

VH Regal Station wagon.

The VH Valiant series, the most ambitious to date, was released in June 1971.

With this model, Chrysler not only gave Valiant buyers a new body (at last!), but went one better and gave them a completely Australian design. It reintroduced the rounded look to a range that had become more angular with every release.

Company executives claimed that four years' work and $22 million had gone into the VH range. They confidently stated that the new model would create such a hit that Chrysler would quickly lift its market share from 12 per cent to 15 per cent — and keep it rising. Certainly the reaction was strong. The press wrote volumes and the dealers reported record showroom traffic.

At 4900 mm (192.7 inches) the VH was only a fraction longer than the previous model. The wheelbase, however, had been increased by 76 mm to 2810 mm (111 inches) and the car was 100 mm wider. The new model was not only the roomiest Valiant up to now, it also looked it. In fact, it looked gigantic!

Chrysler was selling size, while GM-H was taking the other tack. The Holden HQ, due in July, was an open secret: a car which looked smaller than it really was. Only time would tell which company had made the right move.

The Valiant's cleaner lines were strengthened by a big reduction in body decoration and such features as recessed door handles. There was an increased curvature of the front bumper bar; the front parking lights and turn signal lights were moulded to fit flushly above it.

An unusual (for the early 1970s) hatch-type bonnet allowed engineers to add a cross-member above the grille and strengthen the car's front section. The curved rear deck contained a bigger boot than before, the spare wheel was set deep into the floor, the fuel-filler was hidden behind the rear numberplate.

A major complaint was that the new body had less glass area than the VG. Vision was not good; in fact, the car was a parking nightmare. And in spite of the size, there was not an overabundance of leg room or head room.

The new Valiant models were about 45 kg (100 lbs) heavier than their predecessors. They had a completely new interior to go with the restyled body. The instrument panel and dashboard were completely remoulded, the steering wheel and seats were new and the trim featured new patterns. For the first time, pre-moulded carpet was fitted.

Chrysler said:

'The Hemi engine was originally designed for the VH Valiant but completion of Chrysler's engine plant at Lonsdale (SA), enabled it to be brought in and proved in the 1970 VG models.

'The Hemi's success has vindicated Chrysler's belief that a six-cylinder engine with V-8 power meets the requirements of Australian drivers.'

VH buyers were offered four versions of the Hemi engine. The two new Hemis were the '265', a 4.3-litre (265 cubic inches) two-barrel version producing 152 kW (203 bhp) and a high-performance version of the same engine for the Pacer sporting sedan, producing 162 kW (218 bhp). The standard 4-litre '245' and the 'Slant Six' replacement engine, the 3.53-litre '215', were carried over to the new range. The 5.2-litre (318 cubic inches) V-8 was retained as an option on the Regal models.

Unfortunately, in manual Valiants the Hemi engines were mated to the same old three-speed box without a reverse lock-out. The dual-braking system introduced in the VE was included on all VH models with front disc brakes standard on almost all Valiants (excepting the low-compression, standard fuel 215-engined 'fleet special', which represented just 3 per cent of total Valiant production).

Other new features included a floor-mounted handbrake lever on the right-hand side of the driver's seat. A steering-column lock was now standard but this was a fiddly affair which was worked by the driver engaging reverse (in manual) or park (in auto) and then turning the key. This locked the steering and the gearlever and met an Australian standard due in 1972.

All the Valiants had what was described as 'remodelled suspension tuned to the power and aerodynamic qualities of the cars'. The system still consisted of front torsion bars and semielliptic rear springs. Anti-roll bars were fitted to the Pacer, Regal 770 and all station wagon models.

The standard tyre width was now 140 mm (5 inches) instead of 127 mm (5 inches). Fuel tank capacity was raised 20 litres to 89 litres (19.5 gallons). All models had increased soundproofing.

With the new bodies came new names. The medium-line Valiant was called Ranger and the better-equipped version Valiant Ranger XL. The Ranger was identified by its grille of horizontal aluminium bars, rectangular headlights and centrally-placed Ranger ornament.

Ranger buyers had the choice between the 215 and 245 Hemi engines.

The Ranger XL was sold as a car designed to 'bridge the sales gap between economy cars and more expensive models'. It was distinguished by XL badges, wheel trim rings under the hubcaps and mouldings framing the door windows. White side-walled tyres and chrome frames around the tail-lights were other features.

The XL trim was plusher, with a centre armrest and retractable front seat belts, courtesy light switches on all doors and an illuminated boot. Buyers had a choice between the Hemi 245 and Hemi 265. Power assistance for the front disc brakes was optional.

The VH wagon, which was about 152 mm (6 inches) longer than the sedan, had an interior of almost ballroom proportions. It provided the largest cargo capacity of any Australian-built wagon.

Inside the new Regal.

The Regal 770

The 'new look' from behind (Modern Motor).

Valiant's new wagon featured an integral air deflector mounted over the rear window and designed to keep it clear of road grime and dispel exhaust fumes. The Regal and Ranger XL models featured an electrically powered tailgate window, operated by the tailgate lock key or a switch on the instrument panel.

The new Pacer sedan was described by its maker as 'one of the most strikingly beautiful cars of sporting type available anywhere'.

The Pacer, which in VG form had won 17 out of 20 races in its class in 1970, now came armed with the 'hot' 265 engine. This was coupled to a heavy-duty clutch and special gearbox and differential. The Pacer was equipped with different gear ratios to the standard Valiant for quicker acceleration. It outperformed GM-H's V-8.

The Pacer featured a special grille of red bars in a black surround. A wide black stripe ran from midway on the front door to the rear end of the car, where it blended with the black paint treatment of the rear deck and quarter panels. A '265 Hemi Engine' identification was fitted to the rear quarter panels.

The Pacer had high-backed bucket seats incorporating headrests and an instrument cluster painted dark blue with a tachometer amongst its rounded dials. A new gearshift knob design adorned the Pacer's three-speed manual floor control. 165 mm (6 inches) styled steel wheels with 185 S.R. radial-ply tyres were standard.

The VH Regal became the top-of-the-line Valiant entry in the prestige market, with the Regal 770 having a stronger sporting accent. The Regal had automatic transmission and other standard features including an electric clock. Chrysler announced that this model was aimed at the 'the upper 30 per cent' of the Australian market.

On the exterior, the Regal had an engine bonnet ornament, sill mouldings beneath the doors, a wide applique-panel linking the tail-lights and a distinctive paint treatment on its hubcaps. The Regal emblem also appeared on the roof pillar behind the rear door.

Seating included reclining front bucket seats with high backs, incorporating headrests. There were armrests front and rear, plus lights in the glove box, ashtray and under each side of the instrument panel in addition to the usual dome light on the roof. The dome light could be operated by a switch on each door.

The Regal buyer had the choice between rne Hemi 245 (123 kW/165 bhp), Hemi 265 (152

kW/203 bhp) and Chrysler's '318' V-8 engine (172 kW/230 bhp).

Externally, the Regal 770 was distinguished from the Regal by a set of quartz-halogen driving lights mounted between the headlights. It also had overriders on the rear bumpers plus special road wheels and 165 mm (6 inches) steel-belted radial tyres. The trim had a unique basketweave pattern.

With the 770, the Hemi 265 engine (coupled to automatic transmission) was standard and the 318 V-8 optional. A front anti-roll bar was fitted.

Prices started at $2895 for the base 215 Ranger and $2985 for the 245. The 265 two-barrel model was priced at $3235, as was the Pacer. 'Airtemp' air-conditioning was a $400 option.

The Regal 770 sold from $3885. The top-of-the-line Regal 770 V-8 sedan was $4015 and the wagon $4125.

Interestingly, the Valiant's basic price had risen only about 11 per cent since its introduction in 1962, despite the inclusion of many new accessory items and mandatory safety equipment. In the same time, the people building Valiants had gained about 57 per cent in increased pay, steel had gone up by 30 per cent and housing by 25 per cent. An

improvement in production techniques was the main factor in keeping the Valiant retail price down.

Meanwhile the Valiant model line-up continued to become more and more complicated as the year progressed.

Not content with giving the Australian public this batch of new models, Chrysler raised the number of variants to fifteen. This was done by introducing the sensational Charger in August and the Chrysler limousine in November (these models are covered under separate headings).

The other Valiant variant was the two-door Hardtop, released in October 1971 at a price only $70 above the sedan. While the VG Hardtop had used imported panels (and cost about $200 more than the sedan), the new VH Hardtop was built entirely from panels pressed at the company's South Australian stamping plant.

The VH Hardtop was 114 mm (4 inches) wider than the VG version but was about 76 mm shorter. Its length of 4880 (196.6 inches) made it about 100 mm longer than the VH sedan. The boot was the biggest of any Australian production car.

The VH Hardtop was released in Regal and Regal 770 form, both corresponding to the

VALIANT PACER 265
PERFORMANCE

Piston speed at max bhp . . . . . (997 m/min) 29.44 ft/min
Top gear mph per 1000 rpm . . . . (34.6 kph) 21.6
Engine rpm at max speed 5300
Lbs (laden) per gross bhp (power-to-weight) . . (6.6 kg) 14.5
MAXIMUM SPEEDS:
Fastest run . . . . (187 kph) 116 mph
Average of all runs . . . .(186 mph) 115 mph
Speedometer indication, fastest run . . . (180 kph) 112 mph

IN GEARS:
1st . . . . (68 kph) 42 mph (5200 rpm)
2nd . . . . (119 kph) 74 mph (5200 rpm)
3rd . . . . (187 kph) 116 mph (5300 rpm)

ACCELERATION (through gears):
0-30 mph . . . . .3.0 sec
0-40 mph . . . . .4.3 sec
0-50 mph . . . . .6.2 sec
0-60 mph . . . . .8.3 sec
0-70 mph . . . . 10.5 sec
0-80 mph . . . . 14.5 sec
0-90 mph . . . . 18.8 sec

	2nd gear	3rd gear
20-40 mph	3.9	5.8
30-50 mph	3.7	5.8
40-60 mph	3.8	6.1
50-70 mph	3.9	6.1

STANDING QUARTER MILE:
Fastest run . . . . .15.9 sec
Average all runs . . . . 16 sec
BRAKING:
From 30 mph to 0 . . . . .1.6 sec
From 60 mph to 0 . . . . .3.1 sec
ENGINE:
Bore and stroke . .99.3 mm (3.91 in.) x 93.5 mm (3.68 in.)
Cubic capacity . . . . .4340 cc (265 cu in.)
Compression ratio . . . . .9.5 to 1

Carburettor . . . . Carter two-barrel downdraught
Power at rpm . . . . 218 bhp at 4800 rpm
Torque at rpm . . . . . (37.4 kg/m) 273 lb/ft at 3000 rpm
Fuel consumption overall . . . . 16.3 mpg
TRANSMISSION:
Type . . . . three-speed manual, all syncro
Clutch . . . . .sdp
Gear lever location .floor
RATIOS:

	Direct	Overall	mph per 1000 rpm
1st	2.71	8.75	8.0
2nd	1.55	5.00	13.8
3rd	1.00	3.23	21.6
Final drive	3.23		

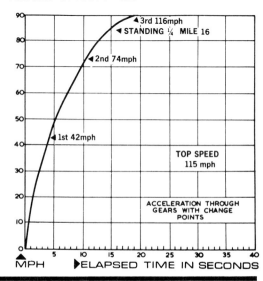

◀ 3rd 116mph
◀ STANDING ¼ MILE 16
◀ 2nd 74mph
◀ 1st 42mph

TOP SPEED
115 mph

ACCELERATION THROUGH GEARS WITH CHANGE POINTS

MPH ▶ELAPSED TIME IN SECONDS

sedan equivalents in equipment level and mechanical specifications. The Hardtop models came equipped with wind-down rear quarter windows and a unique dashboard with round dials set in a fake wood-grain panel. They were priced between $3835 and $4165.

Chrysler put a lot of effort into the VH Hardtop but it was a sales flop. One reason was that the exterior was enormous though inside there was only moderate room, but the main thing was simply that the vast majority of buyers preferred the Charger.

Chrysler had hoped to keep the traditional conservative Valiant Hardtop buyer with this model and win over a new, younger market with the Charger. But it was not to be and people started dubbing the rarely seen Hardtop 'Chrysler's other two-door'.

Despite Chrysler's claim that the VH Valiant opened a new era in quality of finish, there were severe build problems with the 1971 models. These included poor rust-protection, windscreen leakage, timing chain wear, oil leaks and automatic gearbox problems. Although most of these bugs were ironed out by 1972, the damage had been done and the car's reputation had suffered.

Meanwhile there was one more addition to the range. In April 1972 the 'Town and Country' utility was released. Based on the VH sedan, it had a vinyl roof, 'black-out' paint treatment and the 245 Hemi engine.

In June 1972 a four-speed Borg Warner manual gearbox was made available on the Pacer and Charger.

By 1973 over 50 VH Valiant variants were in the VH range. Including 'Chrysler by Chrysler' and Charger models, 67 800 VH Valiants were made.

The VH Hardtop.

The Valiant Book 97

New models, new engines, new concept . . .

VALIANT'S BEST YET!

Bigger and better really do apply this time . . . trim, fittings, paintwork and finish is all vastly improved in the new VHs. Room, comfort, stability and braking leaps ahead too. And then there's the new 203 bhp 265 CID — with the rakish hardtop, VIP and stove-hot Bathurst two-door still to come. By MEL NICHOLS, who was the first journalist to drive the new Valiants . . .

SPECIFICATIONS		
	VH	VG
Length	192.7''	192.3''
Width	74.2''	69.7''
Height	55.4''	55.0''
Wheelbase	111.0''	108.0''
Front track	58.3''	57.9''
Rear track	58.7''	56.3''
Weight	3120 lb	2890 lb
Wheel rim width	5.5''	5.0''
Fuel tank	19.5 gal	15 gal

NO ONE — not even the Valiant dealers — was ready for the shock Chrysler has created with its new VH range.

All the attention was focused on the HQ Holden everyone knew was coming at the middle of the year, and even on the forthcoming Falcon that hits in February. Their styling, engines and specifications were no real secret even six months ago.

But not so with the Valiants. They were a mystery — and so strongly had the Holden captured the spotlight that not even the guessing games were very intense.

Now Chrysler has lifted off the wraps (pulling off a nice little piece of one-upmanship by easily beating GM-H's release) — and it is a bombshell.

The styling is the biggest surprise — it's totally new, totally Australian — a massive departure from previous Valiants which have been little more than American Valiants with different badges, grilles and tail lights.

But there are important new developments among the specifications, engines and equipment too:

Three inches have been added into the wheelbase, but the overall length commendably increases only four-tenths of an inch.

The front track is four-tenths of an inch wider and the rear track up by 2.4 inches — making the Valiant the only "big-three" car with the rear track wider than the front. This development teams with new 5.5-inch wide rims — 6.5 on Pacer and Regal 770 (up half an inch) for better ride and stability.

An all-new 265 CID six that gives 203 bhp at 4800 rpm and a massive 262 lb/ft of torque at 2000 rpm, making it more powerful than Holden's 253 V8 and way ahead of Ford's 250 Two-barrel. It required a new block casting to take the bore from 3.76 to 3.91 in. and uses pistons from the 318 V8 engine.

Disc brakes are now standard on all but the cheapest, small-engined

Bold, wide look VH Valiant owes nothing to previous styling. Wedge shape follows through from wrap-around parking lights to C-pillar. It's adventurous and beautiful.

Right:
Regal wins friends in prestige bracket with its clean, simple lines, lack of ornamentation.

Ranger XL interior gets carpets, central fold-down armrest, rates as Chrysler's big hope in medium class.

WHEELS, August, 1971

Ranger. On Regal and Regal 770 the discs are power assisted.

Inside there's a steering lock, reversible keys, exceptionally good seat belts and the handbrake is now mounted on the floor beside the right-hand side of the driver's seat. Heater controls have been moved over to the right-hand side of the steering column for much easier operation.

The basic model line-up is: Ranger 215/245, Ranger XL, Regal, Regal 770 and Pacer 265. Prices are up $90 over the VG.

The Ranger XL is a brand new model slotted trim, equipment and prestige-wise between the Ranger and the Regal to put Chrysler into more direct competition with Ford and Holden.

The base car, the Ranger 215 (140 bhp) at $2888, is the equivalent of the Holden Kingswood. Chrysler expects most to be sold with the optional 245 160 bhp engine (and the then mandatory disc brakes) for an extra $90.

Then comes the Ranger XL which is the most important of the new models. At $3158 it costs $180 more than the Ranger 245, and goes into direct competition with the Falcon Futura in a slot just below the Holden Premier. It is expected to be the big seller of the range.

It gets the 245 CID six with disc brakes as a standard (but no power assistance) and all the equipment and trim that was standard on the old VG Regal (carpets, split front bench with fold-down armrest, better instrumentation, boot light, night and day mirror and other dress-up gear). The new 265 engine is optional for an extra $70.

The new Regal is $3678, another $265 over the Ranger XL 245 automatic (auto is standard in the Regal). It gets another lot of jazz-up gear that takes it close to the old Regal 770 standard.

And the new Regal 770 goes another step again — not only does it get more snob equipment like a new wood grain instrument panel, but handling and performance gear

as well to make it a real one-up prestige/performance machine at $3878.

The new gear the 770 gets that wasn't on the old VG 770 includes a front anti-sway bar, good-looking ROH 6.5-inch specially-styled wheels taken from the Pacer with 185 x 14 radials standard, two quartz halogen driving lights mounted in the grille and the 265 engine as standard (the 318 V8 is still optional).

The Pacer, with wild body stripes and screaming new colors, is also a big improvement on the old car. It is $88 dearer than the VG Pacer, but gets a new, high-performance version of the 265 engine that puts out 218 bhp at 4800 rpm (20 more than VG's undisclosed figure) and 273 lb/ft of torque at 3000 rpm (28 lb/ft more than the VG).

But there's no four-speed gear-box — it's still a close ratio three-speed driving a high-performance 3.23 diff. A $95

"comfort pack" giving carpets, reclining buckets, three-spoke sports steering wheel and dressed-up instrumentation. The 6.5-in. sports wheels and 185 radials are standard.

WHEELS pulled off the first drive of the new cars — brief though it was — weeks before the release. We drove a Ranger XL 245 manual, Ranger 245 wagon and a Pacer with the comfort pack.

Apart from the styling which, in our opinion looks very good although the glass area has been reduced considerably, the first thing that hits you about the VH is a surprising quality-sounding "thoonk" as the doors shut. It is a sound usually found only on Jaguars, BMWs and Mercedes.

The seats in all but the basic Ranger are good, and the driving

Below left:
Pacer goes all the way with fully calibrated gauges, sporty steering wheel. Gear change still lacks reverse gear lock out.

Below:
Regal drops central padded strip of Ranger and Pacer for bigger dials. Regal 770 gets tacho in place of clock, gives VH a total of four different dashboards.

position above average for this type of car. But the reduced glass area means vision is far below past Valiant standards — the top of the screen is too low and the heavy pillars and quarter vents make side and rear vision correspondingly poor.

The dashboard — also re-styled — is heavily padded on the top edges with the instruments set into a deep, wide nacelle. The steering lock (much like the Austin X6's) is on the column just under the bottom edge of the dash. The steering wheel is still a little high, although not as bad as before and there's a slightly vague feeling in the straight ahead position. But the steering is light with 4.4 turns lock to lock and a 36 ft turning circle.

The gearchange on the manual cars is light and flows well, but there is too much travel. In the Pacer, the floor change still has no real reverse lock-out and it's heavily spring-loaded towards the second/third plane. It is also too notchy.

A good point is the much better rear legroom in all the cars. The foot space is up two inches and the seat is wide and better designed, but headroom is not good enough.

Brake feel was very good in all the cars we drove and the clutches were smooth in the Ranger XL and wagon. But the Pacer's was heavy and tiring.

The new lever handbrake is one of the best ideas we've yet seen on an Australian Big Three car. It is far easier to reach and operate than the old pull-out type.

The Pacer was the only car in which we had even a slight chance of booting along and it revealed exceptionally good performance potential. Quarter times should be in the high fifteens with a top end of more than 120.

The trim, paintwork and finish in more than 20 of the new cars we examined was far better than previous Valiants. It has a definite quality look and feel. The only faults we uncovered were ill-fitting boot and front panels, points that should be corrected on general

Wildly aggressive Pacer accentuates body lines with black stripes. Wide 6½ in. road wheels are standard.

production cars.

The all-new VIP (likely to be called an "Imperial") will not be released until October. It will follow the same styling theme but on a wheelbase in the 116-118-inch region.

But the big news will be with the new hardtop. There will be a special lightweight version (about 2800 lb) for all-out competition and the Hardie-Ferodo 500. The wheelbase will be smaller than the VH sedans, and it will have a wild 275 bhp version of the 265 engine, close ratio three-speed box with a diff around 3.5.

The standard hardtop — which Chrysler claims is fabulously styled — is likely to be called the Challenger or Charger in the American idiom. It will be released in August.

● We'll have full tests on the VHs next month. *

PRICES

Ranger 215 Man	$2888
Ranger 245 Man	$2978
Ranger 215 Man S/wagon	$3088
Ranger XL 245 Man	$3158
Hemi Pacer 265	$3228
Ranger XL 245 Auto	$3413
Valiant Regal 245 Auto	$3678
Valiant Regal 265 Auto	$3748
Regal 770 265 Auto	$3878

OPTIONS

Air conditioning	$400

Power steering	$140 with auto only
Disc brakes	$40 option with 215 engine
Power brakes	$25
Vinyl roof	$70 Ranger XL and Regals
Sure grip diff	$45 Pacer only
Pacer hood patches	$20
Pacer comfort pack	$95
Nylon weave bench seat less	$50 Regal only
245 in lieu of 215 (incl disc brakes)	$90
265 in lieu of 245	$70
318 V8 in lieu of 265	$120

(Continued from page 71)

TECHNICAL DETAILS
VALIANT RANGER 245

MAKE . . . . .Chrysler
MODEL . . . . Valiant Ranger
BODY TYPE . . . . 4-door Sedan
PRICE $2985
OPTIONS . . . . Radio
COLOR . . . . Green Metallic/Green Trim
MILEAGE START . . . . 570 (Pacer 1620)
MILEAGE FINISH . . . . .1009 (Pacer 2587)
WEIGHT . . . . (1415 kg) 3120 lb
FUEL CONSUMPTION:
Overall . . . .(6.8 kpl) 19 mpg
Cruising . . . .(6.8-7.6 kpl) 19-22 mpg
TEST CONDITIONS:
Weather . . . . Cold, clear
Surface . . . . .hot mix
Load . . . . .2 persons
Fuel . . . . Premium
SPEEDOMETER ERROR (mph):

Indicated	30	40	50	60	70	80
Actual	29	39	49	58	68	78

PERFORMANCE

Piston speed at max bhp . . . . .(822 m/min) 2698 ft/min
Top gear mph per 1000 rpm . . . . (38 kph) 23.8
Engine rpm at max speed 4400
Lbs (laden) per gross bhp (power-to-weight) . . (8.6 kg) 18.9
MAXIMUM SPEEDS:
Fastest run . . . . (169 kph) 104.7 mph
Average of all runs . . . . (166 kph) 103 mph
Speedometer indication, fastest run . . . (174 kph) 108 mph
IN GEARS:
1st . . . . (77 kph) 45 mph (5600 rpm)
2nd . . . .(124 kph) 77 mph (5400 rpm)
3rd . . . . (169 kph) 105 mph (4400 rpm)
ACCELERATION (through gears):
0-30 mph . . . . .3.2 sec
0-40 mph . . . . .4.6 sec
0-50 mph . . . . .6.7 sec

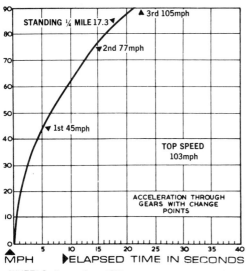

STANDING ¼ MILE 17.3
▲ 3rd 105mph
▼ 2nd 77mph
▼ 1st 45mph
TOP SPEED
103mph
ACCELERATION THROUGH
GEARS WITH CHANGE
POINTS
MPH ▶ELAPSED TIME IN SECONDS

0-60 mph			.10.0 sec
0-70 mph			.13.5 sec
0-80 mph			.20.1 sec
		2nd gear	3rd gear
20-40 mph	. . . . . .	4.1 sec	7.1 sec
30-50 mph	. . . .	4.7 sec	6.6 sec
40-60 mph	. . . . . .	5.2 sec	7.4 sec
50-70 mph	. . . . . .	6.2 sec	9.1 sec

STANDING QUARTER MILE:
Fastest run . . . . .17.2 sec
Average all runs .17.3 sec
BRAKING:
From 30 mph to 0 . . . . .1.2 sec
From 60 mph to 0 . . . . .3.0 sec

SPECIFICATIONS

ENGINE:
Cylinders . . . . .six, in line
Bore and stroke . 95.5 mm (3.76 in.) x 93.5 mm (3.68 in.)
Cubic capacity . . . . .4000 cc (245 cu in.)
Compression ratio . . . . 9.5 to 1
Valves . . . . overhead
Carburettor . . . . Carter single-barrel downdraught
Fuel pump . . . . mechanical
Oil filter . . . . .full flow
Power at rpm . . . . 165 bhp at 4400 rpm
Torque at rpm . . . . . (32.3 kg/m) 235 lb/ft at 1800 rpm
TRANSMISSION:
Type . . . . three speed manual, all syncro
Clutch . . . . .SDP 9.5 in.
Gear lever location . . . . column
RATIOS:

	Direct	Overall	mph per 1000 rpm
1st:	2.95	8.61	8.1 (13 kph)
2nd:	1.69	4.93	14.1 (23 kph)
3rd:	1.00	2.92	23.8 (38 kph)
Final drive	2.92		

CHASSIS AND RUNNING GEAR:
Construction . . . . unitary
Suspension front . . . . independent, unequal length control
arms, Torsion bars (Pacer anti-roll bar)
Suspension rear . . . . . live axle, semi-elliptic leaf springs
Shock absorbers . . . . .telescopic
Steering type . . . . .recirculating ball, ratio 20 to 1
Turns I to I 4.5
Turning circle . . . . .37 ft
Steering wheel diameter . . . . 16 in.
Brakes type . . . . .discs front/drums rear
Dimensions . . . .discs 11 in. (28 cm) Drums 9 in. (22.8 cm)
Friction area . . . . .481.8 sq in.
DIMENSIONS:
Wheelbase .111 in. (282 cm)
Track front . . . . .58.32 in. (148 cm)
Track rear . . . . .58.72 in. (149 cm)
Length . . . . .16 ft 0.7 in. (489 cm)
Width .6 ft 2 in. (188 cm)
Height . . . . .4 ft 7.2 in. (140 cm)
Fuel tank capacity . . . . 19.5 gals (88.5 litres)
TYRES:
Size . . . . 185 x 14
Pressures . . . . F 32/R 30 psi
Make on test car . . . . Uniroyal Radials
GROUND CLEARANCE:
Registered . . . . .6.5 in. (16.5 cm)

CHRYSLER'S Big Guns lined up against the stop watches — and they turned in sparkling performance. But MM Editor Rob Luck also looked at economy, comfort and the condition of the prestige symbol — the Pentastar badge.

CHRYSLER's main objective with the new VH Valiant range was to match Ford and GMH model-for-model in the marketplace. This was the motive behind the model split to Ranger and Ranger XL (matching Belmont/Kingswood, etc.), and it was the biggest single factor behind the expansive new engine range.

Unlike its chief rival at Fishermen's Bend, Melbourne, Chrysler tuned its powerplant range to make it king of the power race. Without question, the company has succeeded — producing a range of six-cylinder engines that from smallest to largest, virtually out-perform every other car in Australia.

For the economy minded, the new small-bore 215 Hemi Six still offers a lusty 140 bhp — as much as The General's biggest six-cylinder gun.

And for the power minded, the new 265 capacity Hemi is offered in basic 203 bhp form or high performance (HP) Hemi Pacer form — 218 bhp.

Chrysler apparently doesn't want to know much about the 215 — the company didn't even put one on its test fleet. We've persuaded them to change their ideas on that one, but while they're preparing a car, we decided to start at the top of the engine range, and bring you a combination test of both 265s — the standard and HP model.

The 265 gets its extra capacity from slicing the bore measurement out to 3.91 in. — all Hemis share the same 3.68 in. stroke, with bore dimensions varying from 3.52 in. on the 215 right up to the 3.91 in. bore of the 265.

The seven-bearing bottom end of this willing mill is well capable of taking the strain, and is efficiently fed from a single two-barrel downdraft carburettor on both 265s (on a split manifold on the Pacer).

Precise horsepower ratings are 203 at 4800 on the 265 and 218 at the same figure on the HP. Torque is massive — 262 lb. ft. at a low 2000 rpm and 273 at a higher 3000 rpm on the HP.

Since the standard Hemi 265 is standard equipment on the Regal 770 and optional on Ranger XL and Regal, developing torque at a lower rpm figure is critical for normal motoring tractability. Even in the Pacer, the torque output is produced at a relatively low figure — though some motoring conditions mean the gearbox ratios have to be used fully for maximum value.

Our two test cars were a fully-equipped Regal automatic sedan ($3775) and a Pacer 265 ($3235). With the steep price increases forced on Chrysler by their expensive new model design and development plus compulsory safety features laid down by Government regulation, these prices fall between the basic model (Ranger manual 215 sedan) at a

REGAL 770 gives you full instrumentation plus other performance accessories like a sway bar and quartz extra lights. Regal 265 as tested gets a clock in the slot where the tacho fits.

steepish $2895 and The Regal 770 318 automatic V8 sedan at $4015.

Additional equipment on our Regal test car, comprised Chrysler air-conditioning ($400), power steering ($140), vinyl roof ($70), and radio (about $100) which lifted the total value of the car to $4485. The Pacer had optional hood patches ($20), interior dress-up pack ($95), Sure-grip axle ($45) and radio (about $100) which put its test value at $3495.

That put us behind the wheel of two pretty pricey packages for performance-orientated machines, so we took a critical look at what the overall package offers before lining up against the stopwatches.

As we showed in the comprehensive model breakdown last month, the Regal offers considerable extra equipment over the Ranger XL — and these extras are all-inclusive in the price. This covers wood grain instrument panel, clock (it kept stopping on the test car), choice of front buckets or nylon and vinyl covered bench seat and centre armrest (we got the latter), monolithic foam-rimmed steering wheel with half-horn-ring, remote control exterior mirror, standard power assistance for the standard brakes, glove box and ashtray lamp, front floor lighting, dual horns and a vanity mirror.

That's packed into a body that is no longer than previous Valiants (looks are deceptive) despite the longer (111 in.) wheelbase. But the body is significantly bulkier — it is almost 5 in. wider to accommodate the bigger track and generous sheet metal work.

Parking-wise, it has some pretty big problems at times. The extra width combines with a greatly increased turn radius to make parking in tight spaces like supermarkets lots an occasional nightmare. The body extremities are extremely difficult to see — a feature that isn't assisted by the very low driving position.

The extra interior space is quite noticeable — and the stylists have given the impression of even greater size merely by clever cockpit layout. Unlike the new HQ Holdens which use deep glass treatment, the Valiant VH is high-waisted with much smaller windows (and not the same degree of visibility) with a seating position that encourages that "enclosed" feeling. Whether you like it or not, depends purely on your personal driving preferences.

Chrysler ran foul of bad publicity early on with both the models we tested. The automatic seat retractors — or inertia-reel style safety belts were having adjustment problems in the hands of inexpert operators, and the Pacer was initially knocked back by registration authorities for an excessive exhaust noise level (as was the more recent Phase Three Falcon GT HO).

The Chrysler inertia reel seat belt is standard on all models from Ranger XL upwards — a very commendable standard fitting that helps push that price upwards. The only other car fitted with this type of belt in

Hemi Action

Australia at present is the fully-imported Volvo 164 — and it uses a different mechanism. On the Volvo, you can trigger the seat belt lock simply by making a very sharp movement — the Valiant system requires an inertial force to displace its trigger mechanism and lock the belt in place.

We rolled the car straight out of the Chrysler Milperra workshops, found a quiet stretch of road and performed several crash stops. The belt performed perfectly every time — although possible brake mal-adjustment enabled us to produce only one straight stop in five. The rest varied from 90 degree slides to a full 180 degree spin.

Later on, when we repeated brake tests during performance evaluations, we tried every type of brake conditioning method to get the car to pull up straight. We warmed the discs by driving with the brakes held on gently, but anything over 75 percent stopping effort produced intermittent rear wheel lock-up — and the inevitable slide.

The Pacer was the same. Five stops for two snaky efforts and a couple of 90 degree slides.

Since Valiant brakes have usually been excellent, we can only assume there was an adjustment problem that put too much braking effort on the rear wheels. Going back to last year's press release of the Pacers at Oran Park, I remember these cars being thrashed by around 30 different drivers including some of the country's top racing men, for literally hundreds of flat-out laps, without experiencing any real brake problems.

And despite the lock-up and spins on our brake tests, the Valiants on this

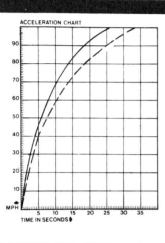

ACCELERATION CHART

MODERN MOTOR road TEST

ROAD TEST DATA SHEET — SPECIFICATIONS

Manufacturer: CHRYSLER AUSTRALIA LIMITED, South Road, Clovelly Park, South Australia.
Make/Model: Valiant Regal 265/Pacer 265.
Body type: 4-door sedan.
Pricing: as tested: $3755/$3235.
Test car supplied by: Chrysler Australia Pty. Ltd., 202 Milperra Road, Milperra, N.S.W.
Mileage start/finish: 2665/3245 : 1478/1595

ENGINE
Cylinders: .... Six, in-line
Bore x stroke: .... 3.90 in. x 3.68 in. (99.7 mm x 93.4 mm)
Capacity: .... 265 cu.in. (4346 cc)
Compression: .... 9.5 to 1
Aspiration: .... Single 2-barrel downdraft
Fuel pump: .... Mechanical
Fuel recommended: .... 100 Octane
Valve gear: .... OHV
Max. power (gross): .... 203 bhp/218 bhp @ 4800 rpm
Max. torque: 262 ft/lb (39.7 kg/m)/273 ft/lb (41.3 kg/m) @ 3000 rpm

TRANSMISSION
Type/locations: ... Automatic/Manual 3-speed all syncro, floor shift
Clutch type: .... sdo

Gear	Direct Ratio	Overall Ratio	MPH/1000	
1st	2.95/2.71	8.6/8.8	9.0	8.8
2nd	1.69/1.55	4.9/5.0	15.7	15.5
3rd	1.00/1.00	2.92/3.23	26.5	24.1
Final drive:				2.92/3.23

CHASSIS AND BODY
Type: .... Unitary
Kerb weight: .... 3170 lb (1441 kg)

SUSPENSION
Front: .... Independent with torsion bars
Rear: .... Four leaf semi-elliptic springs
Shock absorbers: .... Telescopic
Wheels: Regal: .... 5.50 x 14
Pacer: .... 6.50 x 14
Tyres: .... Goodyear Radials 185 SR 14
Pressures: .... 28 lb front 32 lb rear

STEERING
Type: .... Recirculating ball
Ratio: .... 20 to 1
Turns lock to lock: 4½
Wheel diameter: .... 16 in (40 cm)
Turning circle, between kerbs: .... 38.2 ft (11.9 m)

BRAKES
Type: .... Disc front/drum rear
Dimensions: .... 11 in disc (27.9 cm)
Swept area: .... 481.8 sq ins (3083.5 sq cm)

DIMENSIONS
Wheelbase: .... 111 in (281,9 cm
Track, front: .... 58.32 in (148 cm)/59.32 in (151 cm
Rear: .... 58.72 in (149.6 cm)/59.72 in (152.5 cm
Overall length: .... 16 ft 1 in, (491 cm
Width: .... 6 ft 2.2 in, (188.5 cm
Height: .... 4 ft 7.4 in, (140 cm
Ground clearance: .... 6.5 in, (16.5 cm
Overhang front: .... 35 in, (89.5 cm
Rear: .... 48.5 in, (122 cm

EQUIPMENT
Battery: .... 12 V 50 A/
Alternator: .... 35 am
Headlamps: 75/60
Jacking points: .... front and rear bumper

CAPACITIES
Fuel tank: .... 19.5 gallons (88 litre
Engine sump: .... 8.3 pints (4.73 litre
Final drive: .... 2.3 pints (1.3 litre
Gearbox: .... 3.1 pints (1.76 litre
Water system: .... 24 pints (13.2 litre

PERFORMANCE

Test conditions for performance figures; Weather: Fine. Wind: Zer Humidity: 80 percent. Max. Temp: 44 degrees. Surface: D hotmix.

	Regal	Pacer
Top speed, average	104.1 (162.5 kph)	108.6 (173.7 kph)
best run:	108.2 (169.9 kph)	112 (179 kph)
Standing Quarter Mile, average:	17.9 secs	15.9 secs
best run:	17.2 secs	15.6 secs
0-30 mph:	3.5	2.6
0-40 mph:	5.0	3.9
0-50 mph:	7.2	6.6
0-60 mph:	10.3	7.6
0-70 mph:	13.4	10.4
0-80 mph:	18.3	14.1
0-90 mph:	25.2	18.0
0-100 mph:	33.0	26.0

Speeds in gears:

	Regal		Pacer
Gear	Max. mph Drive	Held	
1st	43 mph (68.8 kph)	63 mph (100.8 kph)	45 mph (72 kph)
2nd	70 mph (112 kph)	98 mph (156.8 kph)	80 mph (128 kph)
3rd	108 mph (172.8 kph)		112 mph (179 kph)

test recorded excellent stopping distances and relatively low pedal effort.

If Chrysler is to advertise any aspect of its new model line-up heavily, it should pump the ride and handling hard.

At first impressions, the car seems too squishy — because the ultra-soft ride just irons out all those bumps and the car glides along without very much noise from any source — road, mechanical, or wind. Cross strips and bitumen joins produce a tyre thump occasionally but otherwise the ride is excellent.

Because of that, you'd expect handling to take a dive. But it hasn't. The new Valiants, in fact, have now achieved the best ride/handling combination of the Big Three. The previous criteria was the current Falcon, and the Holden HQ looked set to take over the top honors in this area — but the Holden still leans more heavily on handling with a firmer ride, and the Valiant has the best compromise.

I pounded that big Regal with its floaty power steering down some diabolical dirt and bitumen mountain roads without a single "moment". The

big body leans quite heavily — but that merely helps to keep the passengers isolated from the frantic activity below.

Traction is quite good — you'll get plenty of rear wheel tramp if you use a lot of "foot" on corrugations, but the rear-end generally stays in line, and can be put back properly with power or steering.

The steering on the Pacer was good — firm and positive without being heavy. However, the power steering on the Regal had a disappointing loss of feel once the wheel was turned from the straight-ahead position.

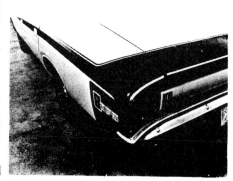

leration holding gears:

	Regal (Drive)	Pacer 1st	2nd	3rd
0	2.9	2.2	3.6	5.4
0	3.3	—	3.6	5.7
0	4.8	—	3.5	5.9
0	5.6	—	4.5	6.3
0	9.2	—	—	6.8

consumption:

	Regal	Pacer
age for test:	13 mpg (4.6 kpl)	16 mpg (5.7 kpl)
recorded:	23 mpg (8.1 kpl)	23 mpg (8.1 kpl)
average:	16 mpg (5.7 kpl)	16 mpg (5.7 kpl)
try cruising:	16-20 mpg (5.7 to 7.2 kpl)	16-22 mpg (5.7 to 7.8 kpl)

flow readings (constant speeds):

ph	24 mpg (8.5 kpl)	28 mpg (10 kpl)
ph	25 mpg (8.9 kpl)	27 mpg (9.9 kpl)
ph	23 mpg (8.1 kpl)	25 mpg (8.5 kpl)
ph	22 mpg (7.8 kpl)	21 mpg (7.5 kpl)

ing: Five crash stops from 60 mph

	G Regal	Pacer	Pedal Regal	Pacer
	.85	.85	10 psi	15 psi
	.80	.90	10 psi	15 psi
	.80	.80	15 psi	18 psi
	.70	.70	15 psi	20 psi
	.80	.70	15 psi	20 psi
mph:	1.8 secs	1.6 secs		
mph:	3.7 secs	4.0 secs		

lated Data:

ton: . . . . .143.3 bhp/ton — 154 bhp/on
n speed at max rpm: . . . . .2982.5 ft/min (903.5 m/min)

do Corrections:

20	30	40	50	60	70	80	90
20	29	39	49	60	70	80	90

RRANTY, INSURANCE, MAINTENANCE, NNING COSTS

stration:

l: Including third party ($40.15) and stamp duty $87.80
: Including third party (40.15) and stamp duty $87.40

ance:

ed rates are for driver over 25 with 60 percent no-claim bonus, where the car is under hire purchase. This is the minimum ium level — decreasing rates of experience, and lower age os may have varying excesses and possible premium loadings.

	Regal	Pacer
Non tarriff company	$69.55	$105.22 approx.
Tariff companies	$71.05	$134.80 approx
NRMA	$76.20	$106.15 approx.

Warranty:

Twelve months or 12,000 miles. Covers all parts and labor charges for defective materials, components or workmanship. Includes components from outside suppliers such as batteries, etc.

Service:

A Service . . . . Free
This covers the first 1000 miles (1500 kilos) and includes lubrication and maintenance service. Materials (oils and greases) are chargeable).
1-15 Services
These are lubrication and maintenance services covering the period from 4000 (6400 kilos) to 60,000 miles (96,000 kilos). These are fully chargeable including labor, materials and replacement parts.
Approximate costs:
$9.75 to $16.90 (1.5 hours to 2.6 hours) labor plus parts.
Oil change every 3000 miles (4800 kilos)
No chassis lubrication

Spare Parts Cost Breakdown:

Front Disc pads $19.26
Windscreen $43.70
Inner front wheel bearings $3.73
Outer front wheel bearings $3.23
Shock absorbers front . . . .$10.08 each
Shock absorbers rear . . . .$10.08 each
At the time of printing, no other prices were available

Workshop Manuals:

Factory manual on all VH models will be available, through Chrysler parts distributors, in August/September and will cost approximately $9.00.

Color range (upholstery colors in brackets):

Regal: Alpine White (gold, tan, blue, black), Ebony Black (tan), Navaho Beige (tan), Deep Chartreuse Metallic (gold, tan), Citron Gold Metallic (tan, black), Sky Blue Metallic (blue, black), Spring Gold Metallic (tan, black), Regency Blue Metallic (tan blue), Russett Metallic (gold, tan).
Pacer: Blonde Olive (tan, black), Hemi Orange (tan, black), Vitamin C (black), Hot Mustard (tan, black).

Minimum garage width:

Measured car width, plus one fully open door 9 ft (374.3 cm)

At straight-and-level, it has a pleasant firm feeling with a nice amount of loading, but the power boosting really takes over as you wind on lock until a really good application of opposite lock leaves you guessing for the location of the front wheels. Experience tells you where — but most drivers will, need time to learn.

Against the stopwatches, both cars put down impressive times — the Pacer very noisily with violent bursts of wheelspin, and screaming rorty engine noises and the Regal with a gentle lunge from the line and smooth, even progress up to top speed.

The dials are still too confusing on the Pacer — Chrysler insists on indicating a red-lettered danger zone on its speedos that looks very similar to the warning area on the tacho.

On the Regal, there's just a speedo to follow — unless you specify the 770 on which the clock is replaced with a much more practical tacho to match up with the other performance extras — quartz halogen driving lights, anti-sway bar, etc.

But the big 265s are a hungry lot. Because I couldn't quite believe the first fuel consumption figures recorded, I ran the most comprehensive set of fuel figures ever on a test car. The fuel flow meter was rarely off either car during the test period, and the crew constantly logged readings in every condition — city traffic, peak-hour conditions, cruising, economy driving, performance testing, country running, etc.

Our fuel measuring equipment allows extremely fine short-distance measurement — down to less than a couple of miles, so the accuracy for any given condition is spot-on.

This is how the figures worked out: Driving for absolute economy, the Regal logged an impressive 23 mpg at a 40 mph average. Its normal high-speed cruising rate was 13-17 mpg and speed variation from average 50 mph to average 80 mph kept the fuel consumption within those extremes. A typical average was 16 mpg for 45 mph average country cruising including hills and overtaking work.

The Pacer proved much more economical — probably the combination of manual gearbox and ideal operating rpm for the fuel system. I was quite surprised to regularly record 23 mpg for city clearway or expressway type condition and 20-22 mpg in light traffic.

Heavy traffic or use of the performance knocked this around quite a bit — to the extent where 16 mpg becomes the normal high speed country cruising average.

However, the constant speed fuel consumption averages shown in the charts prove that the driver with a careful right foot will be well-rewarded with good fuel economy.

There are some detail criticisms of the new Valiants. Probably most important of these is the "feed" or runner system for the inertia reel belts — where the straps loop through their runner thongs to give free movement, the belts often snare and tangle — limiting their efficiency.

Still on the interior — the ashtray needs complete redesigning — it is set at a bad angle, and 50 percent of the times you open it, you'll pull the whole mechanism out and empty ash everywhere. The dash lights blew constantly on the test car — which I eventually traced to loose mounting of the under-dash fuse-box, which has a very flimsy mount. The heater efficiency is also a little slow — allowing early morning misting that's often very hard to clear. Warm-up tim of the engine was also slow.

The headlights could be improve and for some reason the double-side key system for the normal locks hasn been extended to the boot locks.

On the credit side, the silence of th car is quite a remarkable achieveme for the Chrysler engineers and further contribution to the luxury fe of the interior (due to good trim a layout) is the excellent Chrysler rad

Wipers and washers are also ve impressive.

The Big Two-Six-Fives span the ran of high performance a performance/luxury machinery a for that class of car they do a good j at a reasonable price — while st retaining that Chrysler symbol luxury . . . just a notch or so above t average consumer car.

CHARGER (VH)

The Charger XL. PREVIOUS PAGE: Six Pack R/T.

Although released as part of the VH range, the Charger had a life of its own.

It became one of the most remarkable successes in Australian motoring history, and within a scant 12 months, accounted for almost 50 per cent of all Valiant sales.

The Charger was a surprise from the first: surprising styling, surprising price (the base Charger was the cheapest Valiant) and surprising performance. And all this was reflected in sales.

The press reaction was typified by *Australian Motoring News*:

'There can be no denying that the Charger is the most handsome car Chrysler has produced, and probably the best looking car ever produced by an Australian manufacturer. For this reason alone it should be a solid success. . . .'

The Charger was released two months after the VH sedan. It was a time when sales of two-door cars in Australia were running at 20 per cent of the medium-sized car market.

The new model found acceptance among a wide selection of buyers. It has often been called 'Australia's Mustang', not just because the concept of a practical and economical sports machine was similar. Also similar was the wild enthusiasm which marked its release.

Leo Geoghegan, top Chrysler racing driver and Australia's 1970 Gold Star Champion, was closely consulted on the production of the R/T ('Road/Track') version of the Charger. He was also closely identified with the entire Charger line-up from the outset. Upon its release he said:

'It's the best engineered car I have driven. I was amazed by the way the car handles so well without its comfort being reduced in the slightest. It is comfortable enough for Grannie to do her shopping in and smooth enough for her to drive in top gear at 15 miles an hour.

'As for its racetrack performance . . . I can't wait to take on the best competition available in Australia.'

Although the Charger's overall length was 330 mm (13 inches) less than the VH Valiant sedan, it was still a true five-seater, another feature contributing to its sales success. The wheelbase was 2667 mm (105 inches), 152 mm less than the Valiant, and this made for improved handling. The performance was boosted by a 136 kg (300 lbs) weight reduction over the sedan.

The Charger was almost identical to the VH sedan from the windscreen forward. The headlights were rectangular and the indicator lights followed the wrap around style introduced with the VH model Valiants.

The rear-end treatment and roofline were unique. In fact, 60 per cent of the panels was exclusively Charger. The rear spoiler was the first to be built into an Australian car as part of the design. The boot lid — like the bonnet — was of the hatch type. The fuel-filler was located in the upper centre of the rear deck. The body was designed in Australia with some US supervision.

The new model was released in four basic models: Charger, Charger XL, Charger R/T and Charger 770. Each was fitted with a horizontal bar grille with an individualised finish.

The base Charger was very spartan but had the same eye-catching styling as the dearer variations at less than the price of a VH Ranger four-door sedan. It came with the Hemi 215 engine as standard, the Hemi 245 as an option.

With the 215 engine model, the manual transmission was operated by a steering-column lever. With the Hemi 245, the manual transmission had a floor change, while the automatic had a column-mounted selector.

The base Charger's side panelling was distinguished by a feature line beginning in the centre of the door and flaring over the rear panel to join the rear deck and integrated spoiler.

The grille consisted of horizontal aluminium bars with a centre ornament set off by rectangular headlights. The hubcaps featured the Charger emblem. Drum brakes were fitted all round.

The interior was fitted out with high-backed front bucket seats. An optional trim package consisted of floor carpet, rear compartment armrests, instrument panel applique-finishing, wheel trim-rings and pivoting rear quarter windows. A centre cushion armrest between the bucket seats was standard on those Chargers fitted with the Hemi 245.

The Charger XL offered a higher level of standard equipment and, like the Ranger XL sedan, was the most popular choice of its range.

Its 'XL' identity was underlined by styled road wheels with radial-ply tyres, wheel trim-rings

and wheel arch and sill mouldings. Front disc brakes were standard.

In addition to the equipment in the base-line Charger, the XL offered floor carpeting, reclining bucket seats and pivoting rear quarter windows. There was also a remote-controlled exterior rear-view mirror, prismatic interior mirror for night driving and a boot light.

The base engine for the XL was the Hemi 245, the 265 two-barrel (152 kW/203 bhp) was optional. XLs with manual transmission were fitted with a sporting floor-mounted gearshift. Automatics came with the shift lever mounted on the steering column and centre cushion armrests between the bucket seats.

The R/T was pitched at the sporting buyer and also carried Chrysler's hopes of outright victories in Touring Car racing.

The R/T was instantly recognised by its grille of red and black bars with quartz-halogen driving lights mounted between the headlights. A wide black stripe ran from the centre of the door to encompass the rear deck. If stripes weren't enough, the extrovert could order such exterior colours as Hemi Orange, Vitamin C, Hot Mustard, Blonde Olive and Mercury Silver. A centre stripe down the front guards leading from black bonnet patches was optional.

The rear deck was distinguished from the other Chargers by the black paint treatment beneath the spoiler. The car had ventless side door windows and pivoting rear quarter windows. The instruments included a tachometer and an oil pressure gauge. A floor-mounted gearshift was fitted but sadly the gearbox was the inadequate three-speed unit used in previous models.

The R/T's road wheels were made from pressed steel with 165 mm (6 inches) safety rims and radial-ply tyres. A front anti-roll bar was standard.

The R/T's transmission ratios were 2.71/1.55/1.00:1 and the rear axle ratio was 3.23:1, compared to ratios of 2.95/1.69/1.00:1 and 2.92:1 respectively for the Charger and XL models. This change in gearing was to match the high-performance Hemi 265 two-barrel engine which developed 162 kW (218 bhp).

The R/T (and 770) were available with an 'E37' street version of the Six-Pack Charger engine offered for competition cars. The E37 used three Italian-made dual-throated Weber carburettors and developed 186 kW (248 bhp). It was fitted with a full extractor exhaust system.

A full-blown 'E38' racing version of the R/T was

also available. It used a 10.5:1 compression engine which produced 210 kW (280 bhp) at 5000 rpm and 431 Nm (318 lb/ft) of torque at 3700 rpm. It was linked to a transmission ratio of 2.50/1.43/1.00:1.

An additional option with the Six-Pack equipment was the 'Track Pack' which included manual steering with a 16:1 quick-action ratio. A 160-litre (35 gallons) twin-filler fuel tank almost completely filled the boot. Cast-alloy 178 mm (7 inches) rim wheels were fitted with the Track Pack option as was the Sure-Grip anti-slip differential.

With the name 'Chrysler Valiant VH Charger R/T E38 Six-Pack Track Pack', the company put up a strong challenge to the 'General Motors-Holden's LC Holden Torana GTR-XU1' in the marathon names department.

Surprisingly, the E38 came without servo-assistance to its front brakes as standard. Its three-speed box was a limitation not overcome until June 1972 with the release of the R/T E49.

A Chrysler release at the time of the original Six-Pack release said:

'To design the Six-Pack Hemi, Chrysler's top engineers joined the world's foremost carburettor experts from the Italian Weber firm and the company's Australian racing drivers in one of the most extensive programs of its kind ever undertaken.

'The carburettor development alone involved such intricate engineering that a VG Valiant Pacer with the Six-Pack prototype engine was flown 12 000 miles to Europe and then tested for 4000 miles all over Italy.'

Chrysler issued figures showing that the E38 engine produced 48 kW (64.8 bhp) per litre compared with the Falcon 351 V-8's 43 kW (57.5 bhp) and the Torana GTR-XU1's 39 kW (52.5 bhp).

While the carburettor development and tuning were finalised in Italy, the rest of the work on the E38 was done at Chrysler's Lonsdale engine plant.

Engineers had already enlarged the bore of the original Hemi 245 engine from 95.5 mm to 99.3 mm (3.76 to 3.91 inches) for the Pacer and other VH Valiants. This gave it a capacity of 4.4 litres (265 cubic inches). With the increase in bore size came larger inlet valves 49.8 mm (1.96 inches) in diameter. A cast-alloy manifold provided a separate straight inlet tract for each cylinder, so each cylinder was linked to its own carburettor throat.

The Charger R/T coming . . .

Interestingly, one prototype engine was fitted to a special shortened VG utility. The Charger was still a secret, so the ute blazed around the country on extensive trials. Leo Geoghegan tested the Six-Pack ute at the closed Mallala racing circuit (to the surprise of the surrounding farmers) before Chrysler allowed the Charger to be seen.

Chrysler announced the E38 R/T would be driven at Bathurst (see the chapter 'The Valiant on the Race Track') and the R/T E38 'Bathurst Special' was released on 5 August 1971, at a price of $3975. Although the name never appeared on the brochure, this model was presumably the 'Chrysler Valiant VH Charger R/T E38 Six-Pack Track Pack Bathurst Special'.

Less of a mouthful (and handful) was the 770, Charger's luxury derivative.

This was the model which almost totally destroyed the Valiant VH Hardtop's market. It had a plusher interior than other Chargers, a unique grey paint treatment of the front grille and quartz-halogen driving lights mounted between the headlights. It also had a vinyl frame to the side windows, ventless side glass and pivoting rear quarter-windows.

Unique wheel arch and sill mouldings set off its 165 mm (6 inches) styled road wheels, which had radials as standard. The grey paint treatment was extended to the rear, where there were bumper overriders and a dual outlet exhaust system.

The instrument panel (which included a tachometer) had a fake wood-grain finish. Abundant interior lighting was included (in keeping with Chrysler's top-of-the-line fashion). So were reclining bucket seats, soft-grip steering wheel, floor-mounted manual gearshift and console-mounted automatic lever. An anti-roll bar and power-assisted front disc brakes were standard equipment.

Buyers of the 770 had a choice between the 265 high-performance Hemi engine and the 5.2-litre 318 V-8.

The street Six-Pack engine of 186 kW (248 bhp) — as used on the R/T — was also available. It cost an extra $350 and 770s with this engine were fitted with an extractor exhaust system and larger EHR70 radial tyres. They also had distinctive sill mouldings and stroboscopic stripes running along the side panelling.

The Charger prices started at a very low $2795 for the one-barrel 215 Six, rising progressively to $3395 for the R/T 265S two-

. . . and going.

Leo Geoghegan at Bathurst in 1971.

barrel Six (manual). Top of the line was the 770 Automatic 318 V-8, which sold for $4035.

In the value-for-money stakes, every model was a sensation. Not surprisingly, the Charger was an immediate sales success. By October 1971 there was a waiting list of 1800 customers, despite a doubling of production at the company's South Australian assembly plant. Chrysler even reported a strong overseas demand, especially from New Zealand and the UK. Remarkably, 300 Chargers were exported to image-conscious Japanese motorists.

Chrysler had originally decided on a daily production output of 20 Chargers. This proved to be more than a little short of the demand. The press reception was so enthusiastic that production started at 43 a day and had increased to 83 by October. The year finished

with Charger becoming the second (and last) Valiant to win the prestigious *Wheels* magazine 'Car of the Year' award.

In June 1972 there was further action on the Charger front, with the release of a four-speed manual transmission. Made by Borg Warner, the new transmission was said to be the first four-speed gearbox to be totally designed, developed and produced in Australia for a high-powered engine.

It was available as a $155 option for Charger 770, Charger R/T, Charger XL, Charger 245 and Valiant Pacer models. The gear ratios were 2.82/1.84/1.34/1.00:1.

The new gearbox was put to work in a new R/T E49 Charger. This was fitted with the most powerful Hemi yet — a 10:1 compression ratio 226 kW (302 bhp) 265. As standard equipment, the E49 had 178 mm (7 inches) cast-alloy wheels, a 16:1 steering gear, a 3.5:1 Sure-Grip differential and special rear springs and shock absorbers.

The E49 was released at the time of the so-called 'Supercar' controversy. This was a points-scoring exercise in which various politicians (and self-appointed protectors of the public) jumped up and down and foamed at the mouth about the new breed of 'lethal road-registered racing cars'. Car buffs hit back with a call to 'ban low-performance drivers not high-performance cars', but the damage was done. In the wake of political pressure, Holden shelved its proposed Torana XU1 V-8 and Ford pulled the plug on the GT/HO Phase Four Falcon.

Chrysler went ahead and released the E49, a genuine 120 mph-plus (192 km/h) speed machine, but it was to be the last really 'hot' Valiant.

The E49 was the fastest-accelerating production car ever made in Australia. It could reach 60 miles an hour (100 km/h) from rest in a shade over 6 seconds and 100 mph (161 km/h) in just 14.1 seconds. That made it a fair bit quicker than the E38, which was no slug.

The E49 was identified only by a '4' decal on the guard and incorporated a few minor interior improvements such as seat rails designed to lift the front seating position. The 160-litre (35 gallons) fuel tank with dual fillers was an option.

Chrysler announced an initial production run of 200 E49s with the promise that additional units would be built in response to customer orders.

In late October 1972 the Charger 770SE 340 E55 V-8 was released without any song and dance from Chrysler. Still nervous about 'Supercars', the company quietly gave buyers a new Charger with a street version of the 340 racing engine.

The V-8, however, was not strictly a performance machine. It was more a 'grand tourer', sold in luxury 770 trim with more refinement than the R/T and with the fully imported US TorqueFlite automatic transmission as standard. No manual versions were sold.

The E55 engine was fitted with a four-barrel carburettor and produced 206 kW (275 bhp) at 5000 rpm.

(NB: Chargers built after the VH series are described under VJ, VK and CL Valiant model headings.)

The Charger 770 V-8.

CHARGER...

what a steed

AS 179 became *the* catchcry in 1964, so, too, will E38 in '71-72. And you can bet your boots on that!

We say this without hesitation after a rushed, through-the-night test in Chrysler's most powerful Charger R/T — a 1000-mile dash across the spearing straights and snaking hills from Adelaide to Sydney.

We left Adelaide with open minds — and arrived in Sydney totally impressed. This Charger, the full-house competition R/T E38, is a magnificent motor car.

It is not just a race-breed special but a genuine high performance touring machine. It is in fact the first real driver's car Chrysler Australia has ever built.

Until this test we were sceptical about the Charger muscle car. We had driven a couple of examples with very few miles on the clock. They were sorely in need of a tune, and displayed all the idiosyncrasies you'd expect from a high-output race car.

But our finely tuned test car came through the rigors of 1000 miles full bore testing with a constant idle and unchanging per-

formance and flexibility. If any thing, the car was faster at the end than at the beginning of the test.

As our story last month said, the R/T E38 is a development of the Charger purely for Bathurst — but it is more than suitable for the road. The entire Charger range deserves close scrutiny but for this test we wanted to examine the Charger running in the 500.

Chrysler's advertising campaign for Charger has been astonishingly successful. In fact it may have been too clever. It seems the public is only aware of the two model extremes — the price-leading Charger with 215 engine and drum brakes, which lists for $2795, and the racing version, which at $3975 must go close to losing money for Chrysler, but nothing in between.

The Charger concept of a sport-

ing, aggressively good-looking short wheelbase coupe, largely based on the bigger sedan to keep costs down, is certain to prove successful, but if the RT can win races with all the rub off that entails then the company will have worked a minor miracle.

Of course this isn't Chrysler's first crack at the youth market or the race track. The Pacer proved a useful lever in opening the gates to the enthusiast market, but just as the car only ever won its class — with minor exceptions -- so the big sedan was limited in its appeal.

The Charger is a different horse. In the market place and on the track it is a winner.

We collected our E38 from experimental engineer Ken Paddick, in Adelaide, who explained the tyre pressures — F 28, R 26 psi — were set up for near neutral handling, while the suspension was on the softer of the two available settings. Leo Geoghegan — whose role in the development of the E38 cannot be underestimated — likes the firm setting for racing with its tendency to oversteer.

Paddick knew what he was about. These tyre pressures are perfect for the road and suspension. For that matter the whole car was beautifully set-up for quick motoring.

Before charging off into the sunset we walked around our Mercury Silver E38 admiring its stunning good looks. From three-quarters rear it takes on a wildly exciting appearance. It is only from the front that the debt it owes to VH is easily recognised. Overall, while wishing there could have been greater Charger identity up front, the car is a tribute to Chrysler's Australian stylist.

CHARGER — WHAT A STEED

Our car had the marvellous ROH seven inch mag wheels for safety and stability at high and racing speeds and, also, as an added styling attraction. Thankfully it lacked the dealer installed dummy bonnet scoop.

Inside, looking through the windscreen there is nothing to distinguish the E38 from a VH Pacer with the optional comfort pack. And behind the front buckets the short wheelbase isn't easy to pick — rear seat leg and knee room are surprisingly good. Headroom loses out a little but the fairly short cushion is mounted close to the floor so it is possible for two adults to sit comfortably for a fair distance although we wouldn't want to do an interstate trip in the rear.

AND THE CHARGER is only the second of four full model line-ups Chrysler will release in '71. Now comes the Hardtop — for the only official pic yet released turn back to our cover — on the long 115 in. wheelbase which will also be used for the forthcoming Chrysler. The four inch increase in wheelbase is also reflected in overall length, otherwise the Hardtop is virtually identical to the VH sedans. Rear seat room should be outstanding for a two-door car.

The model range has been trimmed. Base Hardtop is a Regal 245 auto with Regal 265 auto, Regal 770 265 auto and Regal 770 318 auto taking it into the luxury bracket. There won't be a manual version. The new 360 cubic inch V8 is being saved for the Chrysler. Prices will be $150 up on comparable sedans.

Anyway in the E38 you need the rear seat for luggage space. The huge 35-gallon petrol tank occupies most of the boot. Between the tank and the rear of the car stands the spare wheel so all that's left are two small pockets on either side of the wheel. Enough room for soft bags, small boxes but little else. The other Chargers run a 17.5 gallon tank — two gallons down on the VH sedans. The sleek styling ribs which run down almost to the spoiler are plainly visible from the driver's seat.

Start the engine, check the 1000 rpm idle and you find it hard to believe there can be three twin-choke Webers feeding the hemi. The gearchange is that same heavy, notchy change you'd gladly swap for something easier on the hand and it still shifts a three speeder and lacks a reverse gear lockout.

The E38's twin plate clutch is not as heavy as you expected but strong enough to build muscles in the left leg driving in traffic jams. It's quite smooth in action but tends to be either in or out.

Big surprise is the steering — even with the high gearing it's light and superbly direct, so direct it takes a few miles before the driver is completely at home. All the slack we complained about in the VH has gone. After driving this who could buy any Valiant without the 16 to 1 (instead of 20 to 1) steering? But the turns lock to lock hadn't been reduced by as much as we'd expected. The VH has 4.5 turns — before checking we'd have sworn the E38 had (at the most) 3.5. A roadside test revealed four turns so it is simply the old steering without the ¼ of turn slack in each direction.

The steering still feels a little dead but it is such an advance over previous Valiant systems we don't feel inclined to knock it. Those who drive R/Ts in competition are going to welcome the change.

Initially the engine feels like any old Pacer unit. It is surprisingly flexible and smooth and perfectly happy to glide along at 35 mph in top gear. Just once or twice before clearing Adelaide we gave the accelerator a decent push with instant results. The

Charger is perfectly named — the E38 lifts its nose and surges forward.

Away from the confines of the city the E38 really came into its own. The compromise three-speed gearbox (there will be a four-speed unit in March next year) is disguised by the engine's immense power and smooth torque. The engine runs smoothly at 1000 rpm but it is not until 2500 rpm comes up that the car really starts to go, and then it runs to 6000 rpm — 1000 rpm beyond the redline but absolutely safe according to Paddick.

But as Chrysler suggests in its excellent little "Hemi/Weber Six Pack" booklet, which comes with the car, owners who intend towing a caravan or pottering around town would be better off with the E37 with its mild cam.

Where the normal two-barrel Pacer engine runs into valve thrash at above 4000 rpm the E38 engine dispenses with this problem altogether, even if it does get noisy above the redline.

After checking out the speedometer for error (it reads slow) we began to run figures on the deserted straights leading north. We expected the Charger to be quick but even our educated guesses were pessimistic.

Over the standing quarter mile the Charger is fractionally slower than the Phase Three Falcon GT HO.

We achieved a best time of 14.8 seconds on a non-skid surface which makes clean take-offs almost impossible unless you bang the clutch home with 6000 rpm on the tacho. On smoother surfaces later in the trip the Charger galloped away so easily that a best of 14.5 seconds is within reach.

It is here the limitations of the three-speed box are most apparent. If a four-speeder were fitted, with a lower first ratio, getting away would be simple regardless of the road surface. A slightly higher top gear would give the car the long legs of a HO or 350 Monaro. All things are relative, of course, for the Charger will cruise happily at a genuine 110-115 mph or around 5000 rpm in top.

But on the open road the three-speed box is able to cope with any situation. A simple down change to second and all the engine's vast performance reserves can be transferred to the road. Up to 90 mph the Charger stays with and in some areas is ahead of the HO — need we say more. Above that the extra cog and V8 power begin to tell but even so the Charger's time of 16.5 seconds to the ton is outstanding from a six-cylinder, five-seater coupe.

Above 110 mph the car begins to slow down although we were still able to record a 100-120 top gear acceleration time. Which brings us to the top speed. After collating speedometer, tachometer and timing checks we have no hesitation in saying the Charger is a 130 mph car.

Given slightly favorable conditions it would run to 5900-6000 in top which gives it a best of close to 136 mph. And 140 mph would seem to be entirely possible down Conrod straight during the 500.

Overall we averaged 13.6 mpg with a best figure in the low 14s and worst in the low 13s. You couldn't really expect more than 16 mpg but that is rather better than the HOs 10 mpg and gives a good 400 mile touring range.

Close ratio gears — close anyway for a three-speed box — give a top speed of 55 mph in first and 95 mph in second at 6000 rpm although from 5200 rpm the gear lever gets the rattles. Even so we didn't use the box all that often, even in twisty country, because the change is so stiff and tiring. Going back to second isn't so bad but the long and heavy shift from second into first takes time and in the long run it is probably quicker to leave the Charger in second.

But all can be forgiven — the E38 is so quick you never seem to drop into a first gear situation on the road because the Charger is far more than just a straight line boomer. It is a superb handling sports machine.

The handling/roadholding/ride compromise is close to perfect and in a different league altogether to the VH Pacer. The Charger improves upon the Pacer's excellent roadholding but the tight steering, firm but comfortable and quiet ride and lack of body roll give it a point to point ability few cars possess.

The steering is generally neutral with a tendency towards oversteer when really booting the Charger along. But this is at speeds no sane person would ever use on the road. Just a flick of the wheel gets the car around most corners; applying more power simply means using less steering lock.

Our early morning run from Cowra to Bathurst showed the Charger in its true light. Here the road surface isn't very smooth and there are plenty of tight and interesting corners. The Charger didn't put a foot wrong and maintained an average speed of close to 80 mph. There is no sideways stepping on corrugations, no wheelspin out of tight corners, only a car glued to the road and moving.

Braking is up the rest of the car. Initially it is very much, "Hell, we'll never stop in time", because without the power assistance the pedal needs enormous push. Once the discs warm up, though, the brakes are excellent. They pull the car up straight and even a number of successive applications from high speeds failed to show up any fade or wheel lock-up.

However Charger owners who don't venture out on to the track or drive at high speeds would be well advised to fit the optional power assistance.

In most other ways the Charger is just Pacer, although the front bucket seats were mounted slightly higher to improve visibility. On this score the car could do with articulated wipers for greater

From the windscreen forward styling is identical to VH sedan but short wheelbase and coupe styling give Charger a look and character all its own.

There is a filler on either side and they feed into one huge 35 gallon tank. ROH seven inch mags are standard on E38.

Cockpit for a King. Charger RT follows VH Pacer layout but with comfort pack items as standard. Large wheel suits car, adds to driving pleasure.

coverage of the screen. The lack of front quarter vents which the Charger R/T shares with the 770 makes a surprising difference to the vision although it doesn't reduce wind noise to a satisfactory level for high speed cruising.

With the small rear vent windows open — they flip out — there is even more wind noise. Face-level vents and extractors are needed for improved comfort at touring speeds.

The higher seats improve the driver's relationship with the big, padded rim steering wheel. Although at first it seems to be unduly high mounted, after 100 miles or so the driver is more understanding and quite happy with its position. The instruments and controls are straight Pacer with the exception that only the driver's side floor level vents are remotely controlled.

There is still no headlight flasher and the clutch pedal is too close to the transmission tunnel to allow the driver's left leg to find a comfortable resting place apart from under the pedal itself.

The buckets are very comfortable, even after 1000 miles, and have excellent lateral support down low — essential really with the "G" forces the Charger can reach — but not enough at shoulder level. We appreciate the penetrating horns and the lights although the small built-in driving lights were set too high and seem to spread their beam to the sides.

As we said at the beginning of this test this is a superb car and one which Chrysler can be proud of. Seldom has the staff of WHEELS been so unanimous in its praise of a new car and especially of a new Australian car. The best indication of our feelings towards the E38 is that even after driving from Adelaide to Sydney in one session we wanted to keep going, to continue to enjoy this virile, responsive and beautifully balanced car. E38 is for the enthusiast. Let's hope the other Chargers at least approach the same standard.

*

(Continued from page 91)

TECHNICAL DETAILS
CHRYSLER CHARGER RT E38

MAKE . . . . .Chrysler
MODEL . . . . Charger RT E38
BODY TYPE . . . . .Coupe
PRICE $3975
OPTIONS . . . . Radio
COLOR . . . . Mercury Silver
MILEAGE START .1068
MILEAGE FINISH 2125
WEIGHT . . . . (1327 kg) 2930 lb
FUEL CONSUMPTION:
Overall . . . .(4.8 kpl) 13.6 mpg
Cruising . . . .(4.3-5.1 kpl) 12-16 mpg
TEST CONDITIONS:
Weather . . . . fine, cool
Surface . . . . hot mix
Load . . . . 2 persons
Fuel . . . . Premium
SPEEDOMETER ERROR:

Indicated mph:							
30	40	50	60	70	80	90	100
Actual mph:							
29	40	50	61	72	82	93	103

PERFORMANCE

Piston speed at max bhp . . . . . (935 m/min) 3066 ft/min
Top gear mph per 1000 rpm . . . . (36.5 kph) 22.7
Engine rpm at max speed . . . . .5600 rpm
Lbs (laden) per gross bhp (power-to-weight) . . (4.7 kg) 10.4
MAXIMUM SPEEDS:
Fastest run . . . . (212 kph) 132 mph
Average of all runs . . . . (205 kph) 128 mph
Speedometer indication, fastest run . . . (205 kph) 128 mph
IN GEARS:
1st . . . . (88 kph) 55 mph (6000 rpm)
2nd . . . . (152 kph) 95 mph (6000 rpm)
3rd . . . . (205 kph) 128 mph (5600 rpm)
ACCELERATION (through gears):
0-30 mph . . . . 2.6 sec
0-40 mph . . . . 3.6 sec

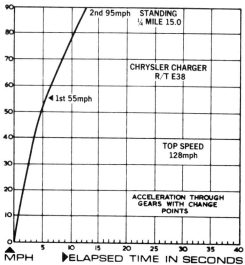

CHRYSLER CHARGER R/T E38

ACCELERATION THROUGH GEARS WITH CHANGE POINTS

MPH ▶ELAPSED TIME IN SECONDS

0-50 mph	. . . . . .	. . . . . .	. . . . . .	4.8 sec
0-60 mph				6.3 sec
0-70 mph				8.2 sec
0-80 mph				10.2 sec
0-90 mph				12.7 sec
0-100 mph				16.5 sec

	1st gear	2nd gear	3rd gear
20-40 mph:	1.9	–	
30-50 mph:	2.2	3.7	7.3
40-60 mph:	–	3.8	6.2
50-70 mph:	–	3.9	5.5
60-80 mph:	–	4.2	5.8
70-90 mph:	–	5.5	7.1
80-100 mph:	–	–	7.3
90-110 mph:	–	–	8.3
100-120 mph:	–	–	13.5

STANDING QUARTER MILE:
Fastest run . . . . .14.8 sec
Average all runs . . . . .15.0 sec
BRAKING:
From 30 mph to 0 . . . . .1.3 sec
From 60 mph to 0 . . . . .3.3 sec

SPECIFICATIONS

ENGINE:
Cylinders . . . . .6 in line
Bore and stroke · 99.31 mm (3.91 in.) x 93.47 mm (3.68 in.)
Cubic capacity . . . . .4340 cc (265 cu in.)
Compression ratio . . . . 10.0 to 1
Valves . . . . .OHV
Carburettor . . . . .3 Weber 45 DCOE
Fuel Pump . . . . mechanical
Oil filter . . . . .full flow
Power at rpm . . . . 280 bhp at 5000 rpm
Torque at rpm . . . . .318 lb/ft at 3700 rpm
TRANSMISSION:
Type .3-speed manual
Clutch . . . . dual plate, diaphragm spring
Gear lever location . . . . floor, centre
RATIOS:

	Direct	Overall	mph per 1000 rpm
1st:	2.50	8.075	9.1
2nd:	1.43	4.612	15.9
3rd:	1.00	3.230	22.7

CHASSIS AND RUNNING GEAR:
Construction . . . . unitary
Suspension front: Independent, torsion bars, unequal length control arms, anti-roll bar
Suspension rear . . . . . live axle, semi-elliptic leaf springs
Shock absorbers . . . . .telescopic
Steering type . . . . recirculating ball, 16.0:1 ratio
Turns l to l 4.0
Turning circle . . . . 36 ft (10.9 m)
Steering wheel diameter . . . . 16.25 in.
Brakes type .disc/drum
Dimensions . . . . .11 in. disc, 9 in. drum
Friction area . . . . 481 sq in. (315 sq cm)
DIMENSIONS:
Wheelbase . . . . .105 in. (267 cm)
Track front . . . . 4 ft 11.32 in. (150.7 cm)
Track rear . . . . 4 ft 11.72 in. (151.6 cm)
Length . . . . 14 ft 11.5 in. (457 cm)
Width . . . . .6 ft 2.2 in. (188 cm)
Height . . . . .4 ft 6.1 in. (137 cm)
Fuel tank capacity . . . . 35 gallons (159 litres)
TYRES:
Size ER70H14
Pressures . . . . F 28 psi, R 26 psi
Make on test car . . . . Goodyear Grand Rally
GROUND CLEARANCE:
Registered . . . . .6.5 in. (16.5 cm)

HOW THE CHARGER SHAPE EVOLVED

Styling sketches show basic Charger shape hasn't changed since pencil first touched paper late in 1969. No. 1 has built-in wing at tail and lacks ribs running from roofline to tail. No. 2 is closest to final Charger except for horizontal tail lights, here it was called Challenger. No. 3 has interesting rear quarter window shape and curving tail lights and No. 4 has triangular rear quarter windows and almost production style tail lights.

AND NOW OUR TEST CREW TELLS...
HERE'S HOW THEY GO ON THE ROAD

WHEN WE JUMPED into our first Charger to drive it back from Adelaide to Sydney it was immediately obvious to our staff a new era had dawned for Chrysler Australia.

Within a few miles in that car — an E38 — we discovered that here was a car that did almost everything right.

Sure, we'd known months beforehand that there was a new

two-door sporty Valiant coming. But to be honest, we must say we'd never suspected this might be The Car Of The Year — it was just going to be another Valiant.

But that E38 planted the seed.

Now in an evaluation of the entire range we have logged 5260 miles in Valiant Chargers — E38, 770 V8, XL 265 and base 245. This covered two interstate runs, extensive rough and dirt road work, continuous city commuting, some track testing and a long searching session at the Castlereagh drag strip taking performance figures and evaluating handling.

It has been a thorough and critical examination of the entire range and now we've positively established its capabilities. We had to be sure of the Charger's merits — and now we are.

After the E38 anything would have been a let-down but the others contained all the same basic

elements of excellence.

Chrysler has tried hard to establish an image with the Charger and, Bathurst apart, it has succeeded. The plan was to have a car to suit everyone — in much the same way as Ford promoted the Mustang in 1964 — for the Charger is to the Valiant what the Mustang was to the Falcon.

And it seems it will be just as successful. There is now a waiting list of 1800 buyers for Chargers.

Above Right: Storming Charger 770 goes well on gravel roads. Normally excellent steering betrays low gearing only on tight situations. Front anti-roll bar is only difference in suspension over XL.

Right: Chargers on the strip: Our twin test revealed startling performance similarities between 770 V8 and XL 265. Both returned best quarter time of 16.7 seconds through the traps.

wheels ROAD TEST

Photography: Uwe Kuessner

HERE'S HOW THEY GO ON THE ROAD

Originally Chrysler planned to produce the car at the rate of 20 per day, dealer and press reaction was so enthusiastic this figure was lifted to 43 when production began but it has since been taken to 83 a day which still isn't enough to meet the demand.

It's not hard to understand why.

We wanted to make sure our judgment was right on the ball so we invited experienced racing drivers to take the wheel only to have an instant confirmation. Even our secretary had a turn and was delighted at the car's ease and responsiveness although her initial reaction was to be scared off by the racey appearance and high performance image.

Our first thought, after driving the VH Valiant Ranger, was it would make an excellent Regal 770. We should also have said an excellent Charger. Shortening the wheelbase by six inches and chopping 13.2 inches from the overall length has had the effect of tightening the entire car. Even the base 245 Charger feels far happier on the road than the equivalent sedan.

The shorter car has meant a reduction in weight of 300 lb per model with an obvious increase in performance. It would have been even more but the pillarless construction means the floor-pan comes in for additional strengthening. From the windscreen and firewall forward, the Charger is identical to the VH sedans.

Continued

Below: Chrysler's 318 V8 punches out 230 bhp but delivers performance of 265 six. Air conditioning drags away some power but six rates high on performance-per-dollar basis.

Right: Crash stop gets front wheel lock-up but car remains straight without rear axle tramp. Power assisted discs have progressive feel, allowing short stops without smoking dramatics.

Left: XL instruments are identical to those in sedan, only the alloy steering wheel spokes show it's a Charger. Automatic selector is hard to read over top of column.

Right: Superb reclining buckets are common to all Chargers except the base model. Comfort level is outstanding even in interstate run. Big three-spoke steering wheel is mounted high.

HOW THEY GO ON THE ROAD

From there back it is quite different. The doors are shared with the VH Hardtop but the rest is unique to the Charger.

The car looks best in its more exotic forms. The 770 and the RT have wide sports wheels and seem to sit lower. Clever use of bright metal work breaks up the high waist line so there is less emphasis on the stubby tail. In relation to its width, the Charger is rather short — not surprising since it is still as wide as the much longer VH sedan.

But the blunt tail with its inbuilt spoiler and roofline ribs running down past the rear window gives the sporting impression the stylists have obviously aimed for. It does not have the beautifully integrated styling of the Monaro — it's more in the boy-racer idiom — but it gets the message across. Perhaps the only real failing is the excessive number of tail light lenses which clutter the tail.

At the front the identity of the Charger is harder to establish but costing considerations meant Chrysler was forced to use the VH grille and panels. Even so it requires just one quick glimpse of the side to pick it for a Charger.

Any Charger looks its best in bright colors — some of Chrysler's present range are positively dull.

After our initial enthusiasm for the RT we were keen to give the others a hard work-out. The first to be delivered to our car park was the 770 in V8 form and fully optioned to include air conditioning. This is one car which does exactly what it was intended to do. It can be a luxurious personal car for a pretty young thing or a high performance touring machine for a red-blooded executive. It is what the Monaro LS should have been.

Chrysler's 318 V8 is not a high revving, brute horsepower engine but it does deliver a smooth flow of power over a wide rev range without running out of breath at the top end.

Its performance to 70 mph is so close to the standard 265 automatic, fitted to the XL we tested, it is easy to understand why the demand for the V8

Rear compartment is surprisingly roomy considering short 105 inch wheelbase. Seat is best for two, will take a third on hard, over transmission tunnel area. Opening rear windows, are standard on all but base model.

engine has fallen off.

Order a standard 770 and you get the RT six which develops 218 bhp, 15 more than the standard 265. The six cylinder 770, therefore, is going to be quicker in most conditions than the V8. And there are the added attractions of better fuel consumption, lower insurance rating, and much lower initial price.

Run side by side on the same day, our 770 V8 and XL 265 returned almost identical acceleration times to 70 mph. The six was only 1.2 seconds behind the 100 mph — a clear enough indication of the performance per dollar built-in to the Charger and, for that matter, the entire Valiant range.

Over the standing quarter mile, the 770 ran through in 16.7 seconds. The XL achieved a best time of 17.0 seconds in drive range and 16.7 seconds when the gears were changed manually. Going beyond the automatic change up points in the 770 just made things slower — an indication of the good engine/transmission combination.

In drive, the V8 slides into second at 40 mph (4100 rpm) and into top at 76 mph (4400 rpm) and goes on to 115 mph. The XL changes up, not quite as smoothly, at 44 and 70 in drive, manually it can be taken to 60 and 95. However, the engine is then getting breathless and there is no point going beyond 50 and 80 for peak acceleration. In the V8, at the redline of 5000 rpm, the car goes to 52 and 88 mph. With no tachometer — and no redline — to watch, the six's inherent ability to rev out makes for its higher speeds. It is so close to the V8 at the top end it does not matter.

The greater torque of the V8 gives it added lift above 70 mph. Even so the 265 engine is so strong the XL feels and goes like a high performance V8 between 40 and 70 mph and only really slackens off at around 90 mph. Low down in the passing range and using the kickdown, the XL surprisingly enough is quicker, admittedly by only fractions of a second, than the V8.

Since both cars use the same automatic transmission ratios and the same high final drive ratio (2.92) the performance is entirely comparable. Only the power-robbing air conditioning unit lowers the V8 figures. It doesn't take long to realise the 265, even without the hp option, is a performance bargain. For just over $3000 you get a five-six seater coupe with a 0-60 mph time of 9.1 seconds.

And like the RT E38 this is not just a straight line drag machine. Both the 770 and XL flatter the driver with an easy, safe and consistent understeer. The addition of the anti-roll bar on the 770 certainly adds

to the driving pleasure of the 770. Although it shares the same steering ratio with the XL it feels far more direct and responsive. The XL tends to have the vagueness we complained of in the VH sedans, but the short wheelbase and firmer springs reduce it to a much more acceptable level.

The steering on the 770 was good — even when parking it remained light — and the feedback of information is outstanding for a recirculating ball system. We were surprised to find it didn't have the E38's higher ratio. Only the weak or stupid would want to fit Chrysler's lifeless power steering to the Charger — and that anti-roll should be standard on every Valiant.

The understeer is hardly noticeable on the 770 until you really start to punt the car hard. Until then the steering is virtually neutral. Once in the realm of nine-tenths driving, the front end does run wide and extra steering lock is needed. Only once, on a sharp down hill gravel corner did the understeer get out of hand. A rapid back-off, down shuffle to second and a big boot swung the tail out, confirming the car's outstanding handling.

XL motoring might not be as precise, but by setting the car up early for a corner and powering through it is almost as quick point to point without being quite as enjoyable to drive. However, in city commuting the XL's throttle response and light steering are ideal. On very tight corners it can spin an inside rear wheel, but it is not really the sort of car you drive this way. In every other circumstance, the power reaches the ground without dramatics.

Both test cars came with Chrysler progressive power assisted discs. They pulled the cars up consistently from 80 mph without lock-up. Only towards the end of a 1500 mile test did the brakes on the 770 give any indication of the gruelling pounding. Pedal travel increased and became spongy after a couple of hard stops, but it quietly returned to normal.

The 770 is quite happy to cruise at 100 mph indicated (both speedometers displayed a commendable accuracy — spot-on at 60 mph and only two mph out at the ton). However, the suspension becomes soft and on one severe bump it actually bottomed at the rear. A 400 mile trip at high speed returned 15-16 mpg from the 770 and in similar conditions the XL gave 18-20 mpg, excellent figures considering the performance.

The ride is superior on the Charger to the VH sedans. The harshness through the steering wheel has gone. Some noise is still transmitted to the cabin, but the ride on the 770 in particular is almost in the European class with a real ability to soak up bumps without jarring the occupants.

Much of the credit for this must go to the seats which are perfectly in phase with the suspension. The buckets on both the 770 and XL are identical to those on the RT and that is high praise indeed. They are on the low side so you tend to grip the bottom of the steering wheel, but even so the driving position is excellent. The reclining buckets have good thigh and lateral support. This doesn't extend all the way up the sides of the squab, but the high backs serve as excellent head restraints.

The XL's seats are divided by a fold down armrest and seat separator which also serves as a cushion when the armrest is pushed back to form a squab. This gives the car a six passenger capacity if necessary for there is surprising room in the rear compartment. The seats in the back are shaped in twin buckets, but what appears to be an armrest is only a dummy. Vast knee room is all that is missing, but there is enough of that to keep two six foot passengers happy for hundreds of miles and three adults can be accommodated on shorter trips. *(Continued overleaf)*

WHEELS, January, 1972

On the 770 the buckets are separated by a console containing the automatic selector and a long glove compartment, the lid for which is spring loaded so that it needs to be held open. It also has sharp edges which only too easily cut a driver's hand. We did notice that the buckets tend to slip back a notch during a long drive. The automatic transmission selector lever contains a button which must be pushed in before you can pick up second or first and this can be annoying when you want a lower gear in a hurry.

Our 770 ran to the same large three-spoke steering wheel which seems to suit the character of the car. Apart from this the interior is virtually the same as the 770 sedan. The wood grained instrument panel contains a full set of instruments, including a tachometer, although these can be difficult to read. The calibrations are too fine and they tend to reflect sunlight. The padded top of the dashboard also reflects into the lower edge of the windscreen and this proved annoying on a long trip driving into the sun.

Tastefully padded door trim, good quality carpeting and a generally solid feel about the interior all make this a pleasant car to be in as well as to drive. Chrysler's awareness of the trend away from black interiors means the 770 has a light tan color interior although black and burgundy colors are available. Panel fit, even on our early production test cars, was excellent and the Charger has a tight feel which is missing from the VH sedans. Only the painted metal area on the dashboard in front of the passenger detracts from the high overall impression of quality.

The XL is slightly less luxurious and retains the standard VH instruments with a horizontal speedometer and three small minor gauges. It also gets the normal two spoke steering wheel without the padded rim. More important, the XL is stuck with the

Boot lid opens to reveal large box although spare Wheel does take up usable space. Petrol tank on Charger is 17.5 gallons, two less than sedans.

opening quarter vents which are a source of wind whistle above 60 mph. The RT and 770 run to one sheet of glass for better visibility and lower noise levels, but the water gutter and exterior mirror build up a roar at high speeds.

Seat belt mountings above the small rear window mean the belts drop down over the driver's shoulder — too close to the neck for comfort. The retractable set-up is good, but the belts tend to become twisted in the top mounting bracket.

Charger represents a new era of engineering and marketing sophistication from Tonsley Park. With its entire '71 range, Chrysler returns to the time when its cars were different and just a little more exclusive than the Holdens and Falcons. With the Charger — low price and all — Chrysler has achieved its aims of building a car for everyone — and capturing the youth market at the same time.

Charger — and that is an appropriate name — is a driver's car. It's not perfect, but it's a damn fine machine.

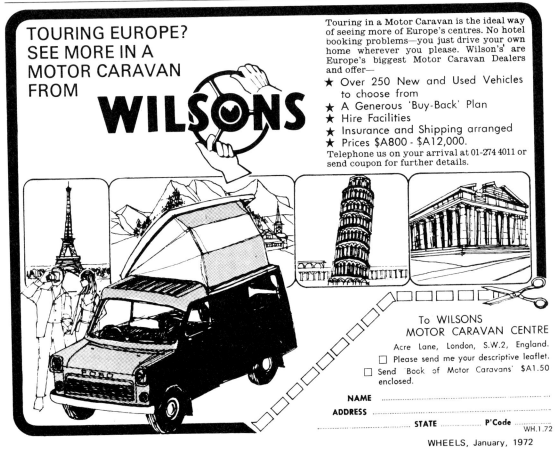

TECHNICAL DETAILS

VALIANT CHARGER XL (770)

MAKE . . . . Valiant
MODEL . . . . Charger XL (770)
BODY TYPE . . . . Coupe
PRICE $3520 ($4035)
OPTIONS . . . . Radio, Radial ply Tyres
COLOR . . . . Metallic Blue (Metallic Green)
TOTAL MILEAGE (TWO CARS) 2314
WEIGHT . . . . 2930 lb
FUEL CONSUMPTION:
Overall . . . . 18.1 (15.3) mpg (6.4 kpl) (5.4 kpl)
Cruising . . . . .17-20 (14-17) mpg
(5.6-7.1 kpl) (4.9-5.6 kpl)

TEST CONDITIONS:
Weather . . . . mild, dry
Surface . . . . .Castlereagh Drag Strip
Load . . . . .two persons
Fuel . . . . Premium
SPEEDOMETER ERROR (mph):

Indicated							
30	40	50	60	70	80	90	100
Actual							
31	40	50	60	70	79	89	98

PERFORMANCE

Piston speed at max bhp . . . . 2777 (2427) ft/min
896 m/min (740 m/min)
Top gear mph per 1000 rpm 23.8
Engine rpm at max speed 4900
Lbs (laden) per gross bhp (power-to-weight) . . . 14.4 (12.7)
MAXIMUM SPEEDS:
Fastest run . . . . .185 (188) kph 115 (117) mph
Average of all runs . . . . . . 183 (185) kph 114 (115) mph
Speedometer indication, fastest run . . . . . . 187 (190) kph
116 (118) mph

IN GEARS:

	Drive (mph)	Held (mph)
1st	44 (40)	60 (52)
2nd	70 (76)	95 (88)
3rd	114 (115)	

ACCELERATION (through gears):

	XL 265	770 V8
0-30 mph	3.5 sec	3.3 sec
0-40 mph	4.9 sec	5.0 sec
0-50 mph	7.0 sec	6.8 sec
0-60 mph	9.2 sec	9.1 sec
0-70 mph	12.4 sec	12.3 sec
0-80 mph	16.2 sec	15.6 sec
0-90 mph	21.2 sec	20.5 sec
0-100 mph	27.5 sec	26.3 sec

KICKDOWN		
	XL	770
20-40 mph	2.4	2.7
30-50 mph	3.3	3.5
40-60 mph	4.5	4.4
50-70 mph	5.0	5.2
60-80 mph	7.3	6.4

STANDING QUARTER MILE:
Fastest run . . . . XL (16.7) 770 (16.7) sec
Average all runs . . . . XL (17.0) 770 (16.8) sec
BRAKING:
From 30 mph to 0 . . . . .1.3 sec
From 60 mph to 0 . . . . .3.4 sec

SPECIFICATIONS

ENGINE:
Cylinders . . . . .six in line (8-vee)
Bore and stroke . . . . . 99.31 (99.31) mm 3.91 (3.91in.) x
93.47 (84.1) mm 3.68 (3.31) in.
Cubic capacity . . . . 4340 (5192) cc, 265 (317) cu in.
Compression ratio . . . . .9.5 (9.2) to 1
Valves . . . . ohv
Carburettor . . . . .single, two barrel, down-draught
Fuel pump . . . . mechanical
Oil filter . . . . .full flow
Power at rpm . . . . 203 (230) bhp at 4800 (4400) rpm
Torque at rpm . . . . .262 (340) lb/ft at 2000 (2400) rpm
TRANSMISSION:
Type . . . . fully automatic, three-speed
Gear lever location . . . . column (console)
RATIOS:

	Direct	Overall	mph per 1000 rpm
1st	2.45	7.15	9.7
2nd	1.45	4.23	16.6
3rd	1.00	2.92	23.8
Final drive	2.92		

CHASSIS AND RUNNING GEAR:
Construction . . . . unitary
Suspension front . . . . . independent, torsion bars, unequal
length control arms (anti-roll bar)
Suspension rear . . . . . . live axle, semi-elliptic leaf springs
Shock absorbers . . . . .telescopic
Steering type . . . . recirculating ball, 20:1 ratio
Turns L to L 4.7 (4.9)
Turning circle . . . . 36 ft (10.9 m)
Steering wheel diameter . . . . 16.25 in.
Brakes type . . . . .disc/drum
Dimensions . . . . 11 in. disc, 9 in. drum
Friction area . . . . 481 sq in. (315 sq cm)
DIMENSIONS:
Wheelbase . . . . .105 in. (267 cm)
Track front . . . . .4 ft 10.32 in. (4 ft 11.32 in.)
150.7 cm
Track rear . . . . .4 ft 10.72 in. (4 ft 11.72 in.)
151.6 cm
Length . . . . 14 ft 11.5 in. (457 cm)
Width . . . . .6 ft 2.2 in. (188 cm)
Height . . . . .4 ft 6.1 in. (137 cm)
Fuel tank capacity . . . . .17.5 (77.5 litres)
TYRES:
Size . . . . 185 SR 14
Pressures . . . . .F 28 psi, R 26 psi
Make on test car . . . . . . .Goodyear Power cushion Radial
GROUND CLEARANCE:
Registered . . . . .6.5 (16.5 cm)

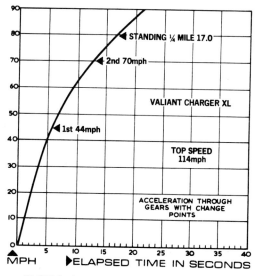

STANDING ¼ MILE 17.0

2nd 70mph

VALIANT CHARGER XL

1st 44mph

TOP SPEED
114mph

ACCELERATION THROUGH
GEARS WITH CHANGE
POINTS

MPH ►ELAPSED TIME IN SECONDS

the last of the supercars

ROB LUCK was the first journalist to slide into the E49 Charger for a full road and track test. His findings suggest that the current Supercar controversy is little more than a sensationalist vote-catching mission by politicians . . . . .

TEST CAR SUPPLIED BY RYDE CHRYSLER, EPPING RD., SYDNEY.

BEING the first to test the *first* of a new series is not new to us at MODERN MOTOR. But being the first to test the *last* of an era is something else again.

It was with considerable regret that we noted the Charger E49 test qualified on the last count.

The Charger E49 will surely go down in automotive history as the last of the Australian Supercars.

They died as they were born — violently. There was about as much sentimentality involved in their execution as is displayed in a Mafia extermination.

They were conceived more than four years ago the direct descendants of pure hard-core stock, but sired out of a totally irresponsible set of race regulations.

They lived in a world of almost day-to-day drama and crisis. They were constantly attacked from every conceivable direction, and somehow, incredibly, they survived.

COLOR PAGE The package almost unchanged visually - but "4" numeral in side stripes gives-away the four-speed '72 car. Handling shows major improvement over last year's car, with greatly reduced understeer tendency and the choice of optional oversteer with power.

They died only weeks ago — cut down almost at the peak of their maturity by the same kind of irresponsibility that led to their initial conception.

The public may well be left confused and bewildered in the aftermath of Cyclone Supercar.

But it's doubtful if they'll be able to forget the E49 — it looks like being the sole survivor of the Supercar era.

Our test E49 came to us in a most unusual fashion. Since Chrysler hasn't really been organised in the business of preparing and providing road test cars for the past three years, it came to us as no surprise to find an "alleged" road test car was not available for test in a four-week period after its registration.

But we found a livewire Chrysler dealership that was prepared to part with an E49 for virtually unlimited testing. The car provided by Ryde Chrysler in Sydney was probably the best prepared test car we have ever received. It was detailed to an incredible degree, and in preparation for our road and track workout, a team of mechanics worked around the clock over a weekend to ensure every aspect of preparation was covered.

The car was set-up for us with th correct jets, and was properly tune electronically. The diff was replace with a limited slip of the correct ratic Brakes and suspension got deta attention to ensure adherence t factory competition specification.

When we rolled out of the worksho on Epping Road headed for Oran Par we felt everything was right. At th same time, we were immediate impressed with the improvemen Chrysler has effected over the old E3

I was probably the fiercest critic c last year's car and I don't think I w proved wrong in any important are It's significant that points which cam under heavy criticism last year see almost beyond reproach this year.

The E49 is a different car fro end-to-end. Of course its basicall built around the new and long-awaite Borg Warner four-speed gearbo which will soon be the regular unit both Australian Chrysler and For products.

It's a good box apparently tou and durable, with a firm, notchy leve short precise movements between th slots and a reverse well protected by lift-out gate.

You can hammer shifts through a occasionally beat the syncro rings a battling down through the gearbox f lower gears you may nick the edge the teeth when you're pushing har

E49.

A three-spoke steering wheel is now standard and it's a really good tiller. Coupled with the 16 to 1 steering gear it gives good feel with a pleasant, precise action. And it's set at a good angle for applying lots of lock.

The only other detail cockpit change is a new simplified ignition/steering column lock. Chrysler's old affair was a bit awkward to operate — the new one is probably the simplest and most effective supplied by any local manufacturer.

Unlike Ford which also produces (or should that read "used to produce") competition vehicles for regular sale, Chrysler is very open with the specifications and price structure of its Charger E49. They've got good reason to be — since the specifications show a sensible balance of performance and safety, and the pricing is remarkably competitive.

You can buy the E49 in two packages, which is described in a rather complicated code. The factory designation reads:

Pack 1 — E49 D20 D56 A87 A95
Pack 2 — E49 D20 D56 A84 A95

A closer look reveals the specification is easily decoded. Looking across two lines you'll see the only difference is under the Acode — the second pack (which is the Bathurst car) has an A84 code which complements the A87 code in the first package. The A84 code simply denotes the use of a 35gallon fuel tank with dual fillers and appropriate bod modifications.

This is how the rest of the message decodes — we've shown the code, with its translation and the relative cost of each item.

	retail inc. tax
E49 — engine	$3465
D20 — trans (4-spd)	$155
D56 — 3.50 lsd	—
A87 — track pack (stand.)	$140
A84 — fuel tank	$20
A95 int. dress-up pack	$95
TOTAL	$4320

Chrysler is equally free with its information on detailed specifications. This is a break-up of the code:

E49 — ENGINE

● 10.0:1 compression ratio.
● Shot-peened larger section con rods.
● Increased piston-skirt-to-bore clearance.
● Fully floating piston pin.
● Molybdenum filled top & intermediate piston rings.
● Shot-peened crankshaft.
● Tri-metal big end bearings.

But basically it's a good, firm box with plenty of precision and a sturdy feel.

And it feels just so bloody marvelous in the E49 after that dreadful three-speed that was inflicted on race-drivers last year.

The fact that it's got a well re-built car wrapped around it helps even more. The E49 has a well-revised suspension system that includes better front-end geometry and revised spring/shocker rates all round.

The result is a firmer, flatter ride, with less of that brutal plough understeer that reduced the handling qualities of last year's E38 and made great gobs of negative camber on the front wheels essential for trackwork.

The E49 actually comes close to the concept of the race car you can drive straight to the track from the showroom floor. I took the test E49 straight from Ryde Chrysler to Oran Park and put down immediate 58.5 second laps on Goodrich radials with 46psi in the tyres.

The best lap set out of six was 58.2 which would have come back to an interesting 56.2 on Goodyear Grand Rallies. With the series lap record at just over 51seconds and racing tyres and blueprinting left to exploit, the potential seems remarkable. The E49 could well be the first production sedan to break the magic 50 second barrier at Oran Park.

And driveability was something else. Unlike the old E38 in which you sat on the floor and tried to peer over the dash, the E49 puts you at the right height (on seat-rails chocked-up by 2in.) in a seat beautifully set-up in relation to the steering wheel and pedals.

Unbelievably, Chrysler has still provided a pedal system that makes heel-toe down-shifting an agonising exercise in callisthenics — and this is accentuated by the continuing lack of power assistance on the brakes.

I still won't wear either Chrysler's or Leo Geoghegan's argument that a boosted system can't provide progressive braking — but I have to take their point that a non-boosted system does. It's virtually impossible to lock the Charger's wheels, unless you're really overdoing the braking, but pedal efforts sometimes in excess of 160lbs means you could wind-up with a telescoped leg.

Thumping away constantly at a heavy set of stoppers must induce fatigue, and this concept I find

undesirable in a long-distance racing car.

It's also unfortunate the E49 is equipped with inertia-reel seat belts. These are quite unsatisfactory for any kind of performance driving, since they provide no lateral location (surely a large part of any seat belt's function). During the track laps, the sideways g-loadings meant that lack of a restraining seat belt limited the driver's control at times.

The seats themselves are great. They are firm with good shaping and they bite into the body to hold you quite firmly in most driving situations. A good seat-belt would ensure they performed well in all situations. Chrysler provides fully adjustable seat-back as standard, and combines with a wide range of fore-aft adjustment, it is difficult to imagine a build of driver who couldn't get comfortable behind the wheel.

Chrysler pioneered head-restraints in this country — at first perhaps a little crudely with the tombstone seats in the early Pacers, but they quickly refined the process to the high standard that first appeared in last year's Chargers.

They have overcome one of the major problems of seat design in two-door cars — the grappling for seat back release levers down on the side of the seat: Chrysler puts a neat chrome button high up on the side of the seat squab to give no-bend access to the rear seats.

Instrumentation is unchanged. It's comprehensive, with dials for tacho and speedo and gauges for temperature, oil pressure, fuel and amps. Chrysler hasn't corrected the shortcomings of last year's cars — tacho and speedo are too confusing, and the oil pressure gauge is still furthest away.

TOP: Up on power, down on oversteer — combined with the four-speed unit, the Chrysler's detailed trackmods make it a big mover for 1972 competition.

RIGHT: Systematic preparation in the well-equipped Ryde Chrysler workshops covered suspension, diff, wheel balancing, engine tuning and other aspects.

BIG STIRRER: Borg Warner's four-shifter is the heart of the E49's 1972 specifications. It has close, fast shift movement, lift-out for reverse.

- Camshaft — 308° duration.
- Shot-peened valve springs.
- Windage tray.
- Large vibration dampers.
- Aluminium intake manifold.
- 3 x 2 BBL 45 DCOE Weber carburettors.
- Unsilenced air filters.
- Dual outlet tuned-length extractors.
- Finned cast alloy rocker cover.
- Dual plate clutch.
- ER70 H14 tyres.

D20 — TRANSMISSION
- Four-speed manual.

D56 — REAR AXLE
- D56 3.50 to 1 'Sure Grip'

A87 — TRACK PACK
- 16 to 1 steering gear.
- Steering column shaft to suit gear.
- 7in. cast alloy wheels.
- Brake modifications:
  (1) Rear brake adjusters deleted.
  (2) Finned rear drums.
    (3) Front disc dust shields deleted.
  (4) Proportioning valve.
  (5) Brake master cylinder special push rod.
- Rear spring rates and associated shock absorbers.
- Rear spring front hanger brackets adjustable.
- Sure grip rear axle.

A84 — TRACK PACK
- This is same as A87 except 35 gallon fuel tank with dual fillers and body modifications to suit.

A95 — INTERIOR DRESS-UP PACKAGE
- Reclining Bucket Seats.
- Carpet.
- Three-Spoke Sport steering wheel.

Chrysler has shown restraint in its external designation of the hot E49 — the only clue you'll get is the figure "4" etched into the vertical black-out stripes on the front guards.

There is a slight (but virtually undetectable) variation in the side stripes and the bonnet black-outs are gone. Otherwise it's stock E38 in appearance.

But it's not stock E38 in performance and handling. Our Charger test car went noticeably harder than last year's Bathurst machine. The E38 I track tested last year was prepared by Chrysler and I ran quick laps in both private testing and in conjunction with racing drivers.

The best the car would turn on Goodyear Grand Rally rubber was 58 seconds flat — a time which this year's car almost achieved on B.F. Goodrich Radial 90s, at least two seconds down on performance.

But the big difference was in the *ease of lapping* — last year's car was a dedicated understeerer that ploughed straight-on even with 10lb fr/rear tyre pressure differential.

The E49 answered the helm well, with strong understeer in the tight hairpin at the end of the straight where you'd expect it, but a generally neutral characteristic in the other corners combined with a willingness to be tossed or powered into oversteer.

A slight application of negative camber and some positive castor would improve the situation still further.

Achieving 58 second laps in last year's car was a fairly "desperate" business. The E49, by contrast, knocked down the same times this year with smooth track manners — always easily within the confines of the bitumen verges.

And surprisingly, the four-speed gearbox played very little part in the track times — since the gear spacings were poorly suited to Oran Park (after all they were designed for Bathurst and there's no similarity in the circuits).

But they were still vastly superior to the three-speed. On the E38, first proved too low and second too high for the two tight corners on Oran Park. With the E49, second slot was just right for the tight bits, but worked out slightly too low for the next section of slightly faster corners — the Esses and Suttons corner.

I tried alternate laps using second (at 5500) and third (well off the redline) for these sections, and this produced equal times. Second was more secure with readily available power on tap, but it was also pushing undesirably close to the engine's limits.

PERFORMANCE
CHARGER R/T E49

Test conditions for performance figures; Weather	Fine
Wind	Gusting 8-16 knots
Humidity:	40 percent
Max. Temp.	58 degrees
Surfaces:	Dry hotmix
Top speed, average:	128 mph (204.8 kph)
best run:	132 mph (211.2 kph) @ 6000 rpm (estimated)
Standing quarter mile, average:	15.7 sec
best run:	15.1 sec
Speed at end of Standing Quarter	92 mph (147.2 kph)
0-30 mph	3.3
0-40 mph	4.2
0-50 mph	5.8
0-60 mph	7.3
0-70 mph	9.4
0-80 mph	11.6
0-90 mph	14.5

Speed in gears:

Gear	Max. mph	(Kph)	rpm
1st	39	64	5000
2nd	61	98	5000
3rd	85	137	5000
4th	112	181	5000

Acceleration holding gears:	2nd	3rd	4th
20-40	3.1	4.8	6.4
30-50	2.8	4.3	6.2
40-60	2.9	3.8	6.3
50-70	2.9	3.8	5.3
60-80	—	4.0	5.0

Braking: Five crash stops from 60 mph

Stop	G	Pedal	Time
1	.8	160lbs	4.3secs
2	.8	200lbs	3.8secs
3	.65	200lbs	4.5secs
4	.65	140lbs	4.2secs
5	.60	125lbs	4.8secs
30-0mph	.7	130lbs	2.0secs

Speedo Corrections:

30	40	50	60	70	80	90
28	38	48	57	67	76	87

E49

CHARGER has always had impressive under-bonnet appearance, but revised air cleaners, new linkages look even more professional on '72 car. Box of dials is Ryde Chrysler tuning kit.

Over the fast Dogleg, third was just coming into its element but tyre limitations prevented me from exploiting the full potential of engine and suspension. With even a medium throttle application, the car started a full slide before the apex that concluded on the extreme outer edge of the track only a fraction before a firm braking application was required for Energol.

My comment from last year's car still stands — the steering wheel is "perfect," with good feel, correct dimensions and great placement for good control.

Braking is the one area that Chrysler should look to for improvement. The car stopped and stopped progressively. But the big discs and rear finned drums just aren't working hard enough.

After six laps of hard braking, they tired quickly on the standard linings,

but even on the first laps they required up to 200lb of pedal effort and still recorded only .4g stopping effort.

Oil pressure remained steady all round the circuit and temperature stayed in the normal operating range.

The acceleration tests showed the car is a dynamic performer off-the-line, with newfound performance from the additional engine modifications. However the extra slot only cuts down on the top-end acceleration times, where our fifth wheel showed a loss of up to half a second for each shift.

Flexibility is really remarkable — and in this respect Chrysler has achieved a standard of engine tuning that is absolutely world class.

The car can actually be trickled away from a standstill in top gear, and pulling away from 15mph with gentle throttle applications is easy. From 25-30mph you can feed the beast full

throttle, and from there on, it's a matter of lying back in the cushy buckets and feeling the surge of acceleration.

Our performance tests were all completed on the racing jets and racing plugs — it's hard to imagine with road gear installed it could be any better. We logged 60 miles through heavy traffic without noting any fussiness. When we reached the track, the car pulled cleanly to 6000rpm in first and second but showed some slight breakdown near the top of the third gear range. This cleared after only two acceleration runs and the car ran faultlessly thereafter.

Chrysler has certainly put together a safe Supercar that makes a mockery of hysterical political mumbo-jumbo aimed at discrediting this concept of car.

The improvement on last year's car is remarkable — we particularly admired the attention to detail that cleared up all our earlier criticisms of finish and assembly. The under-bonnet workmanship was first class.

The improved formula could be just enough to give Chrysler victory at Bathurst. With the demise of the V8 Torana and Ford's Phase Four GTHO Falcon, Chrysler fronts the Mount Panorama grid with the only 1972 Bathurst car — to compete against the 1971 Bathurst cars from rival manufacturers.

Unless more politics get in the way! ∎

The Supercars

hat got away

Comparing Chrysler's E49 six and E55 eight

WHILE GMH and Ford pulled in their horns — and their supercars — Chrysler showed the world the Charger E49, the "fastest six-cylinder" car (to use its words). Then, without even a press release, came a high performance V8 Charger with a mild version of the 340 cid racing engine.

Official public showing of the 770SE 340 E55, as it is known, was at Sydney Motor Show, although WHEELS readers learned all about it exclusively in last month's issue.

Rather than run separate tests on the new E49 and E55 we decided to match the two super versions of the Charger to discover if the V8 can run in the same league as the hot six.

Although both are obviously aimed at the performance oriented buyer, the E49 is strictly a racing car that can be driven on the road while the 340 is an extension of the 770 Charger and directed towards luxury and smoothness with the added acceleration as a bonus.

Chrysler make a direct comparison impossible because the E55 comes only with the fully imported, American Torqueflite automatic transmission and the E49 with the new Borg-Warner four-speed gearbox. This difference in the mechanical specification gives a very good idea of the direction in which Chrysler aimed the concepts of the cars.

Consider the E49 as a pure racing machine and its tractability and top gear performance are outstanding, but it lacks the sheer flexibility and torque of the V8.

Without having to compensate for the three-speed gearbox of the old E38, Chrysler was able to extract even more power from the 265 cid engine by a mild cam tuning.

Pictured at right (top): New facia differs to those in other Chargers, is exclusive to the E55. Speedo and tacho are flanked by two gauges — one for water temperature and charge rate, the other for oil pressure/handbrake warning lights and fuel level. Floorshift automatic transmission is standard on E55. (Centre): 340 V8 engine has four-barrel carb, provides effortless performance which is matched by the car's handling and brakes. Air conditioning is a $440 extra. Power steering is also available, for $140, but the steering is light enough not to need it. (Bottom): Contrasting inlaid panels on seats are also exclusive to the E55 model. Front seat occupants have inertia reel belts. High top anchor point means sash belt tends to rub against wearer's neck.

THE SUPER CARS THAT GOT AWAY

Even so the improvement in performance makes the E4 easily the fastest accelerating car made in Australia, an quicker than the E38 by a significant margin.

One of the major reasons for the new car going so muc faster is the lowering of the rear axle ratio from 3.23 to 3. and this has, of course, helped in the quest for stree tractability. Such is the flexibility of the six that it will pu away strongly from just 1500 rpm in top and go down to a low as 1000 rpm before it starts to grumble.

Real go, however, begins at 3000 rpm. That's when the ca shoots forward at an astonishing rate and you seem to spen more time changing up through the excellent four-spee gearbox than watching for the tacho to spin around to th redline.

Maximum power of 302 bhp is developed at 5400 rpm an torque of 320 lb/ft at 4100 rpm. Chrysler's tacho is redlined a 5000 rpm but it is perfectly safe to go to 6000 rpm althoug we picked 5500 for the change-up point when running th acceleration times.

At these revs the gear maximums are 40, 61, 85 with a to speed of 112 mph so they are spaced almost perfectly for bot track and road use and combine superbly with the torque c the engine.

The lower gearing has detracted from the car's ability as long-distance tourer — this is where the E55 comes into it own — but even so it will maintain 5000 rpm in top gear wit only a bit of gearshift rattle and wind noise intruding, and i will go beyond 6000 rpm if you are game.

But high speed distance running was never really a forte c the old E38. Where the Charger is absolutely unbeatable is i winding mountain country. We don't mean tight hairpi bends, although it is still horribly quick through these, but o fast, open sweepers and meandering switchbacks.

The raw, quivering power is instantaneously on tap an with a ratio for every conceivable situation the Charger jus storms through and it would take a Ferrari Daytona wit racing driver Jack Ickx at the wheel to stay with one.

There is never any doubt that it is a supercar but it is als an incredibly safe and sure supercar. Full power can be pu through to the road at any speed above five mph without th driver being worried about the car going sideways and even i wet conditions it is possible to transfer at least three-quarter of the engine's torque to the road surface and put u staggeringly quick point to point times.

It is only now that we have driven the Charger with th four-speed gearbox that we realise just how much better it over the old three-speed unit, good and all that it was.

Cornering is as close to neutral as is possible and even usin full power to exit a bend the tail doesn't come round quickl You feel the tail sit down in the corner and gently feed th wheel through your hands, millimetre by millimetre as yo correct the change to a gentle power oversteer.

With the fully adjustable suspension, both front and rea some of the old Chargers were incorrectly set-up from th factory and they understeered excessively but the latest tes car showed us just how good they can be if they are properl tuned.

One area which still needs watching are the brakes. Bot the test E49 and E55 came with power-assisted disc and i each instance the brakes could be made to fade badly after couple of stops from 80 mph. The poor quality linings used i the Chargers — and the same comment applies to the Falco GT and Monaro GTS — should be corrected immediately if th manufacturers are serious about primary safety. Anothe problem on the E55 was rear wheel lock-up coming into corner.

After the E49, the E55 seems almost slow in acceleratio until you compare its performance with, say, a Falcon G manual. It is quicker over the quarter-mile and has a simila top speed. Chrysler's performance motoring departmen seemingly has something for everyone.

The E55 340 engine produces 275 bhp at 5000 rpm an 340 lb/ft torque at 3200 rpm and although it is fitted with four-barrel carby the engine is limited by the use of a ca straight from the 318 engine and a restricted exhaust syster

wheels road test
technical details

CHRYSLER VALIANT CHARGER E49/E55

MAKE . . . . CHRYSLER
MODEL . . . . .VALIANT CHARGER E49/E55
BODY TYPE . . . . .Two-door Coupe
PRICE $4300 (E49), $4850 (E55)
OPTIONS . . . . .radio
MILEAGE . . . . .total mileage in two cars — 2641
WEIGHT . . . . 3010 lbs (3260 lbs)

FUEL CONSUMPTION:
Overall . . . . 13.8 (12.9 E55) mpg
Cruising . . . . .13-16 (12-16 E55) mpg

TEST CONDITIONS:
Weather . . . . fine, cool
Surface . . . . Castlereagh dragstrip
Load . . . . .two persons
Fuel . . . . Premium

SPEEDOMETER ERROR:

Indicated mph	30	40	50	60	70	80	90	100
Actual mph	29	39	49	59	69	79	89	100

PERFORMANCE

Piston speed at max bhp . . . . 3434 (2750) ft/min
Top gear mph per 1000 rpm 20.3 (25.0)
Engine rpm at max speed 6500 (4800)
Lbs (laden) per gross bhp (power-to-weight) 9.9 (11.4)

MAXIMUM SPEEDS:
Fastest run .131 (122) mph
Average of all runs . . . . .130 (120) mph
Speedometer indication, fastest run . . . . .132 (125) mph

IN GEARS:

	E49	E55 Drive	E55 Held
1st	40 (5500 rpm)	47 (4500 rpm)	56 (5500 rpm)
2nd	61 (5500 rpm)	77 (4500 rpm)	94 (5500 rpm)
3rd	85 (5500 rpm)		120 (4800 rpm)
4th	112 (5500 rpm)	see text	

ACCELERATION (through gears):

	E49	E55
0-30 mph	2.8 sec	2.9 sec
0-40 mph	3.4 sec	4.2 sec
0-50 mph	4.6 sec	5.7 sec

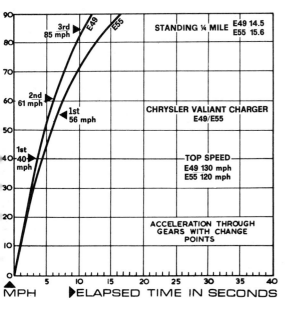

0-60 mph			6.1 sec	7.2 sec
0-70 mph			7.6 sec	9.7 sec
0-80 mph			9.4 sec	12.6 sec
0-90 mph			11.9 sec	16.1 sec
0-100 mph			14.1 sec	21.2 sec

	2nd gear E49	3rd gear E49	4th gear E49	kickdown E55
20-40 mph	2.6 sec	—	—	2.4 sec
30-50 mph	2.4 sec	4.0 sec	6.6 sec	2.5 sec
40-60 mph	2.4 sec	3.2 sec	5.3 sec	3.3 sec
50-70 mph	2.8 sec	3.4 sec	4.2 sec	4.4 sec
60-80 mph		3.3 sec	4.6 sec	5.1 sec
70-90 mph		3.3 sec	4.9 sec	6.6 sec
80-100 mph	—		5.3 sec	8.0 sec

STANDING QUARTER MILE:
Fastest run . . . . 14.4 (E49) 15.5 (E55) sec
Average all runs . . . . 14.5 (E49) 15.6 (E55) sec

BRAKING:
From 30 mph to 0 . . . . .31 ft
From 60 mph to 0 . . . . 145 ft

SPECIFICATIONS
(E55 in brackets)

ENGINE:
Cylinders . . . . six in line (vee eight)
Bore and stroke . . . . .99.3 (102.6) mm 3.91 (4.04) in. x
                    93.5 (84.0) 3.68 (3.31 in.)
Cubic capacity . . . . .4340 (5571) cc 265 (340) cu in.
Compression ratio . . . . .10.0 (8.5) to 1
Valves . . . . ohv
Carburettor . . . . three twin throat Weber (one four-barrel)
Fuel pump . . . . mechanical
Oil filter . . . . .full flow
Power at rpm . . . . 302 (275) bhp at 5600 (5000) rpm
Torque at rpm . . . . 320 (340) lb/ft at 4100 (3200) rpm

TRANSMISSION:
Type . . . . .four-speed manual (three-speed automatic)
Clutch . . . . .dual plate
Gear lever location . . . . .floor

RATIOS:

	Direct	Overall	mph per 1000 rpm
1st	2.82 (2.45)	9.87 (7.15)	7.3 (10.2)
2nd	1.84 (1.45)	6.44 (4.33)	11.1 (17.2)
3rd	1.32 (1.00)	4.62 (2.95)	15.5 (25.0)
4th	1.00	3.50	20.3
Final drive	3.5 (2.92)		

CHASSIS AND RUNNING GEAR:
Construction . . . . unitary
Suspension front . . . . . . independent, torsion bars, anti-roll bar
Suspension rear . . . . . . live axle, leaf springs, adjustable settings
Shock absorbers .telescopic
Steering type . . . . worm and roller
Turns l to l 4.0 (4.7)
Turning circle . . . . 36 ft (10.9 m)
Steering wheel diameter . . . . 16.25 in.
Brakes type . . . . .disc/drum
Dimensions . . . . disc 11.0 in., drum 9.0 in.

DIMENSIONS:
Wheelbase . . . . .105 in. (267 cm)
Track front . . . . 59.32 in. (150.7 cm)
Track rear . . . . 59.72 in. (151.6 cm)
Length . . . . 14 ft 11.5 in. (457 cm)
Width . . . . .6 ft 2.2 in. (188 cm)
Height . . . . .4 ft 6.1 in. (137 cm)
Fuel tank capacity . . . . 17.5 gallons (80 litres)

TYRES:
Size ER7014
Pressures . . . . F 32 psi/R 30 psi
Make on test car . . . . Goodyear Grand Rally

GROUND CLEARANCE:
Registered . . . . .6.5 in. (16.5 cm)

GALVAFROID
fights rust in your car as only zinc can fight it

Just brush it on
...it's galvanised!

which gives an exhaust note similar to a vacuum cleaner under hard acceleration.

The idle is a subdued rumble, as expected from a hot V8, but this pleasant note disappears once underway. Thankfully, the driver is never aware of the lack of a quality noise although pedestrians will be disappointed.

Certainly the 340 is an engine with an enormous development potential. Given even a mild blueprint with improvements to the exhaust manifold and a hotter cam it would have a performance within reach, if not superior to, the E49.

As our acceleration charts show it is not far behind and gets to the ton in just over 21 seconds, quick in all but the fastest company, which includes the E49 — it takes just 14.1 seconds to reach the magic figure.

Where the six-cylinder car really created the speed sensation on the dragstrip the V8 required just a flooring of the accelerator, a chirp of wheelspin and a forward thrust by the car with the driver never aware that it is going as quickly as the 15.5 seconds quarter-mile time indicated.

Here it is one of those wonderful two-faced cars, which are quick without the noise and thunder, which go with the E49 and other similar GT cars. Chrysler offers you the choice.

Suspension settings are virtually identical although softer spring rates are used on the E55. Together with the 20:1 steering ratio, instead of the E49's 16:1 ratio for a reduction in steering turns lock to lock of 4.7 to 4.0, this is the only change under the body. Even the seven inch wide ROH mags are standard on the E55.

Steering response and accuracy are good on both and it is only in tighter sections you begin to want the more direct ratio of the E49. The feedback of information is never really enough but both systems are a significant advance over normal Valiant steering.

When we first drove the E55 we thought it had a superb power steering set-up. A quick check under the bonnet proved otherwise but the beaut steering remained. It is light enough for any woman driver where the E49's steering might become a little heavy in parking situations.

Chrysler's new range of Chargers have cured many of the minor problems which inflicted the old versions, but a couple still remain. However, the seats of the E49 and E55 have been raised at the mounting points and this makes all the difference to the driving position for shorter drivers.

It is now possible to see over the wheel and down onto the bonnet rather than through it and across, so visibility is much better. Also improved is the driving position — short drivers no longer have to hang on to the wheel for support but sit back and direct it. Tall people find it makes little difference to what was an already fine driving position.

The tall bucket seats are still rated excellent with marvellous thigh, lateral and lumbar support. Only the short cushions could bring forth any criticism.

Ride in both is surprisingly comfortable considering their sheet roadholding ability. Joints in concrete or bigger than normal bumps bring on the traditional Chrysler thud but the firmness could never be rated overdone. The compromise on the E55, because of its wider market appeal, has been very successfully achieved, slightly in favor of handling.

Small things like reflection in the right hand instrument panel of the E55, the position of the dipper on the floor, the seat belt location points, the pedals and the controls still leave a lot to be desired. But Chrysler has padded the entire area in front of the passenger so the cheap looking painted metal dashboard has disappeared.

So you have two fine performance machines. Which one? Well it depends on what you want. The E49 is a firebreathing Ferrari-style car while the E55 is more in the Mustang breed with fine looks combined with performance and the ease and comfort of automatic transmission, and even air conditioning, if you so desire.

Both are fine in traffic, although for crowded city areas there is no beating the automatic. To make a choice would be very difficult and we would rather chicken out and have both. One for commuting and the other for our favorite stretch of mountain country.   *

CHRYSLER (1971)

The crew of Modern Motor try the Chrysler on the dirt.

The luxurious 'Chrysler by Chrysler' was released in November 1971 in four-door sedan and two-door Hardtop form.

It took the VIP concept one step further and Chrysler went to even greater lengths to tell the public that this was not a Valiant. It was a luxury limousine by Chrysler. And the best equipped of its type in the world thank you very much!

As to how one classifies cars 'of its type' is not worth exploring but, suffice to say, the equipment level was unusually high.

Strictly speaking, the Chrysler was an appendage to the VH range but it was officially listed as the CH Chrysler.

The styling followed the overall lines of the recently introduced all-Australian Valiant with the addition of a US Dodge-style grille. The overall length was stretched to a fraction under 5000 mm (196.6 inches) and the wheelbase to about 2900 mm (115 inches). It shared this extended length and wheelbase with the Valiant Hardtop (against 4900 mm and 2820 mm for the Valiant sedan).

With a bumper bar encircling the grille and dual headlights, the car was instantly recognisable. The rear treatment had a horizontal tail-light assembly incorporating stop, turn signal and reversing lights of the wraparound type.

Standard equipment included power-assisted steering and front disc brakes, tinted power-operated windows, push-button radio with a power-operated antenna, a carpeted boot and a vast variety of interior lights including adjustable reading lights for the rear compartment passengers. There was also an extraordinary amount of soundproofing.

The instrument panel had what was imaginatively described as a 'Carpathian elm wood' finish. This was the most exotic grain of polyvinyl-chloride yet seen in an Australian car.

The 'Chrysler by Chrysler' hit the showroom floors about six weeks after the company had expected to have it on sale. The main hold-up was the incredible demand for the Charger, which was being pushed off the Tonsley Park line at the maximum volume possible.

Despite the delay, the Chrysler still appeared

The Chrysler Hardtop.

in plenty of time to make an impact. The release came almost five months before Ford had its all-new ZF Fairlane on the market. The newcomer also worried GM-H, which offered less equipment with the Statesman and lacked a two-door variation.

Instant press reaction was to declare the Chrysler 'King of the Big Three Prestige Models'. One of the most talked-about features was the optional electric-powered seat adjuster which allowed the driver to tilt the seat or move it fore or aft and up or down. This cost an extra $125.

The only other options were air-conditioning, an auto-search radio combined with stereo tape-player and a vinyl roof (which was standard on the Hardtop). The vinyl roof was available in three colours — black, parchment and a brown Paisley grain.

Also much talked about was a small light which illuminated the keyhole for 30 seconds after the driver's door had been opened. The front seats were of a US-style split-bench design.

Mechanically, the Chrysler was most notable for its introduction of the '360' engine. This US-designed 5.9-litre (360 cubic inches) V-8, rated at 190 kW (255 bhp), was produced at the Lonsdale plant in South Australia. It was a further development of the Valiant 318 (with larger bore and stroke) and was fitted with a two-barrel carburettor. It added $200 to the price.

Another mechanical bonus was that the Chrysler was fitted with the imported TorqueFlite automatic transmission, rather than the locally produced (and less smooth) unit fitted to Valiants.

Both sedan and Hardtop were offered with a choice of the 265 Hemi. The all-up weight of the Chrysler was a hefty 1077 kg (3570 lbs) but the top speed (for the V-8) was over 175 km/h (109 mph).

Prices started at $4895 for the six-cylinder model and rose to $5872 for the fully optioned V-8.

(The CJ and CK model Chryslers are described under VJ and VK Valiant model headings.)

The Chrysler by Chrysler.

Over the past four years, the full resources of Chrysler Australia have been directed toward a very special goal.

To build Australia's Ultimate Motor Car.

The Chrysler **is** that car.

We do not discuss here, the merits of owning a great luxury car. We assume you have already reached that understanding.

Instead, we simply list the main features.

Exterior Styling

1. Tasteful, aerodynamic wedge styling in a full limousine size.

2. Distinctive looped front bumper, completely enclosing dual headlamps.

3. Formal roof covering of paisley patterned brown vinyl, leathergrain black or parchment. (Standard Hardtop, optional Sedan.)

4. Elegant hand - painted coachline along the full length to enhance the Chrysler's shape.

5. One - piece wrap - around rear bumper incorporates tail-lamp grouping. Side - marker lamps have inlaid castle emblem.

Interior Styling

1. Woven nylon brocade upholstery in Interlaken pattern.

2. Comprehensive instrumentation including ammeter and clock, deep set in Carpathian elm panelling.

3. Spacious interior dimensions: Legroom front, 40.34''; rear, 38.25'' minimum. Headroom front, 39''; rear, 38''. Shoulder room, front and rear, 59.2''.

Comfort Items

1. Exclusive 50/50 split bench front seat design is a Chrysler first. Can be used as a broad one-piece bench seat; or with twin centre arm rests lowered, as two independent 'arm chair buckets'. Each seat has its own armrest, is independently adjustable for legroom and angle of recline.

2. Full width rear seat with fold-down centre arm rest.

3. Specially moulded loop pile carpeting throughout. Carpeted boot and spare wheel.

4. Standard 13 - transistor push-button radio.

5. Options of Airtemp air-conditioning, Searchtune radio, with stereo casette tape player.

Convenience Items

1. Power operated windows, power disc brakes and power radio antenna. Co-axial power steering with built in "road feel".

2. Illuminated boot, glove-box and ash receiver. Twin rear compartment reading lamps, time delay ignition light, 4-door courtesy switches, fender indicator lights.

3. Deep, jet aircraft type, vinyl pockets on the rear of the front seats for rear passenger stowage.

4. Seat belts for all passengers. Front seat harnesses are linked to automatic retractors.

5. Remote control exterior rear view mirror. Prismatic day/night interior rear view mirror.

6. Elegant leather - grain inside door pull handles. Flush mounted pull-type exterior door handles.

7. Anti-theft steering column ignition lock.

Engineering

1. 360 cubic inch Chrysler V8 developing 255 brake horsepower at 4,400 revolutions per minute. Or 265 cubic inch displacement Hemi six cylinder.

2. Smooth 3-speed column mounted "Torqueflite" automatic transmission.

3. Torsion bar front suspension with anti-lean sway bar. 4-leaf semi elliptic spring rear suspension with isolators for noise reduction.

4. Unibody construction using 8,000 individual welds for enormous strength and silence.

Quality Control

1. Double thickness paintwork and sound insulation throughout.

2. 11 additional inspectors devote full time to performing 140 overlapping quality control checks.

3. A 12 mile open road test is carried out in addition to the normal factory road test.

The policy of Chrysler Australia Limited is one of continual improvement in design and manufacture wherever possible to ensure a still finer car. Hence specifications, equipment and prices are subject to change without notice.

CHRYSLER. GREAT IDEAS IN MOTION

CHRYSLER AUSTRALIA LTD.

Two more views of the massive Chrysler Hardtop.

VJ SERIES (1973)

The VJ Regal wagon and (PREVIOUS PAGE) Ranger sedan.

Despite the success of the Charger, Chrysler's overall market share fell slightly in 1972, as it had in 1971, 1970 and 1969.

For the first time, the future of the company was being questioned.

The styling of the sedan — described by Chrysler in 1971 as 'years ahead of its time' — was already thought of as dated and a whole new range of competitors seemed to be snapping at the heels of the Big Three.

Despite this — and the fact that the VJ was only a refinement of the VH — it became the biggest-selling single Valiant model, with 90 865 units sold.

There was no new sheet metal, the styling changes being restricted to the grille, round headlights and revamped tail-lights. The major mechanical improvement was an electronic ignition system which became standard on the Regal, Charger XL and 770 and Chrysler. This was the first time this feature had been offered on an Australian-built car.

Other than that, the VJ was the same old Valiant!

The sales point this time around was not a 'new' Valiant but a better equipped and better built one.

Still reeling from build-quality problems experienced with the VH, Chrysler was determined to fight back and increase its market share. The company was now putting a bigger than ever emphasis on quality control. Advertising focused on new body-finishing techniques (with rustproofing primer) and higher paint application quality.

The cost of offering an enormous range of sedans, coupes, hardtops, wagons, utes and limousines had hurt Chrysler, and with the release of the VJ, the company set about rationalising the range.

The Pacer, Ranger XL, Regal 770 and Charger R/T were dropped with the VJ series. But despite offering only 18 basic models (against 56 for the VH), Chrysler executives felt they could cover the same ground by greatly increasing the option list.

Amongst the small number of changes, new seats were added across the range and a new 'flat' steering wheel fitted. This had the rim flattened at the bottom, supposedly for portly drivers. With the VJ, Chrysler became the first local manufacturer to use a speedometer with metric calibrations.

Like the sedans, the wagons were almost devoid of change. They had a new latch for folding the back seat and a newly designed front bench seat.

The VJ Charger was a big disappointment. Chrysler officials had fought hard for Valiant's low-cost high-performance image, but after the release of the E49, the company didn't want to know about racing or high-performance motoring. The reasons were various; the 'Supercar' controversy and an increasing public concern about long-term fuel supplies were major factors.

The emphasis was now on luxury and quality, which was all very well, but Ford and GM-H were cleaning up much of the Charger's former market with the Falcon Superbird and Holden Monaro.

A surprisingly successful advertising campaign based around the slogan 'Hey Charger' had ensured there was still plenty of interest in Charger (it had easily been Australia's top-selling two-door the previous year), but the lucrative youth market was suddenly shut out of Chrysler's strategy.

The new Charger offered very little in the way of exterior changes. A heavy facelift in the grille department was mainly aimed at making sure people could recognise it from head-on as a different car. The new grille treatment had a pillar effect and 178 mm (7 inches) round headlights. Guard-mounted front turn signal lights with body-coloured bezels were added and the tail-lights were redesigned.

The VJ Charger trim was improved and a larger choice of colours offered. The range was reduced to three basic models (the Charger, Charger XL and Charger 770) but the standard equipment list was improved and the number of options increased.

All Six-Pack and V-8s had a front anti-roll bar and swinging rear quarter windows. Electronic ignition was fitted to all Chargers except the base model with a 215 engine.

A sports pack enabled the buyer to lift the XL to almost VH R/T specs. Sorely missed in the lower priced market was the 163 kW (218 bhp) edition of the 265 Hemi. The Six-Pack and the 318 V-8 were the only powerhouse options.

The Chrysler 'CJ' was announced in March and put on sale in early April. The styling was not greatly changed but the appearance was noticeably improved. The painted coach line was deleted and the sill and wheel arch mouldings — previously available only as an option — became standard. Those cars with vinyl roofs were fitted with lowered mouldings to give the whole car a lowered look.

As before, the Hemi 265 was standard and the 5.9-litre '360' V-8 available as an option.

The commercial vehicle range was 'added to' with the release of a low-budget, Dodge-badged utility which was virtually identical to the Valiant model. The utes had revised grilles and round headlights. The 215 Hemi was standard on both, and the Valiant had a slightly higher level of equipment.

VJ prices started at $2849 for the 215 Valiant four-door. The Regal 245 (with electronic ignition) was $3600, the Chrysler $4925.

Charger prices started at $2970, rising to $3995 for the Charger 770. The 'other two-door', the Regal Hardtop, was $3765. The Dodge ute was $2565, the Valiant ute $2640.

Chrysler finished 1973 with a 9.5 per cent market share — its lowest in memory. For the first time it was behind a Japanese company (Toyota).

In July 1974 the company announced a rise in Valiant equipment levels. Fitted to all models (except utes) were front disc brakes with power booster, front seat retractor safety belts, speed windscreen-wiper blades, a sound-deadening package, door reflectors, a glove-box lock and an anti-roll bar.

August brought the announcement of a limited run of 500 'Charger Sportsman' models. Available only in 'Vintage Red', the Sportsman had bold white exterior striping and a distinctive roof treatment. It was fitted with the Hemi 265 engine coupled to a four-speed manual gearbox. Plaid cloth inserts were in the seat trim and other extras were fitted.

A total of 90 865 VJ Valiants was made.

The VJ Regal.

The Ranger tail-light treatment.

VALIANT RANGER

ABOVE: The 'CJ' Chrysler.
BELOW: The Charger and two-toned Charger Sportsman.

VK SERIES (1975)

In the words of one motoring writer, the release of the VK was a case of 'same tune, new lyrics'.

The VK, like the VJ, was based on the VH. To identify it as a new model, the VK had the customary new grille treatment and revamped tail-light assembly plus a few changes here and there to the ornamentation and nameplates.

Some detail changes were made to the trim and dashboard but it was generally agreed that the Valiant needed a lot more changes than these to compete in the 1975 Australian market. The trend was firmly towards smaller cars.

Chrysler directors called the VK a 'stopgap', claiming that a VL model — with entirely new body panels — was on the way. The problems which had beset the company in the days just before the release of the R Series Valiant had reappeared. Chrysler was stuck with big cars when people wanted something smaller.

1975 was a hard time to sell Valiant-sized cars for a variety of reasons. The 1973-74 fuel crisis had pushed the price of fuel up by 50 per cent; Australians were reacting by ditching their big cars for way below their real value and trying to cram their families into Toyota Corollas or even Chrysler's own Galants.

Family 'Sixes' had once accounted for 70 per cent of the market. By the time the VK was released the figure had slid to 28 per cent.

Chrysler claimed the highlights of the new models were: improved economy and performance, new safety features and major improvements in comfort and driving features.

A move Chrysler officials referred to as a 'rationalisation of models and options' took the model choice down from 11 to eight. These were Chrysler sedan, Regal sedan and wagon, Ranger sedan and wagon, Charger XL and 770, and Dodge utility.

The option list was trimmed in an attempt to make the production line more efficient and reduce the dealer inventories.

Another change was the extension of the use of the name Chrysler for models throughout the Valiant/Chrysler range. The base Valiant and Charger were henceforth known as Chrysler Valiant and Chrysler Charger and their nameplates were revised accordingly. Similarly, in other vehicles which had worn

Valiant badges (Centura, Galant and Lancer), the same shift was made.

All VK Valiant and CK Chrysler models with six-cylinder Hemi engines were equipped with a new Carter two-barrel carburettor. This 'solid-fuel' carburettor was designed to meet US emission requirements and it later helped the Hemi comply with ADR 27A — the clean air law introduced in Australia in 1976.

The VK also brought the release of the 'Fuel Pacer' option. This was the first of those now fairly common vacuum devices which use a flashing light to assist the driver in avoiding fuel wastage. This light was not mounted on the instrument panel as later became usual, but on the right-hand guard, beneath a chrome shield.

The VK safety features included a pressure-sensitive proportioning valve to reduce the possibility of rear-wheel lock-up during braking, power-boosted brakes (as with later VJs) and hazard warning lights. Radial tyres were fitted to the Regal sedan and Charger 770.

Another new feature was a steering column stalk containing controls for the turn signals, windscreen-wipers and washers, headlight dip and headlight flashers. This was the first stalk control from the Big Three. There were also more comfortable seats, new trim styles and colours, courtesy switches on all doors, a quartz clock on the Chrysler and Regal and illuminated heater controls.

The VK Valiant Regal had automatic transmission, reclining bucket seats, centre cushion armrests, heated rear windows and other features. A flowthrough ventilation system was fitted to the sedan, but it was a primitive type without the directional dashboard air vents which some competitors had had for 13 years.

Five Chrysler engines were used. The '360' (5.9-litre) was available as an option on most models, including the Ranger sedan and Charger 770.

VK prices started at $5310 for the base Ranger and rose to $6783 for the 770 V-8. The '265' Charger 770 was $6191, the Chrysler V-8 was $8784.

20 555 VK Valiants were made — the smallest production run since the S Series.

The VK Regal.

The VK Charger — inside and out.

CL SERIES (1976)

Chrysler CL Regal. PREVIOUS PAGE: Chrysler CL Valiant.

Chrysler Australia had promised an all-new Valiant after the 'stopgap' VK model, but this was not to be.

An Australianised edition of the handsome new US Plymouth Volare/Dodge Aspen intermediate-sized sedan had been styled and costed and looked to be a certainty. But by early 1976 Chrysler was forced to tighten its belt and postpone all thoughts of a new car.

As a result, it was 'same tune, new lyrics' time again with the CL Valiant, released on 21 October 1976. Major styling changes gave the Valiant a substantially new look at the front and rear but, again, the car was essentially a remodelled VH.

For the first time in three models however, there was some new sheet metal. The front had a new nose-cone and bonnet. New rear panels included the boot lid, lower panel and quarter panel. A new bumper bar was fitted below the redesigned tail-lights and the fuel-filler cap was relocated in the lower panel of the rear deck.

The revised front and rear treatments were complemented by full wheel covers, sill and door frame mouldings and different ornamentation.

The new CL range continued the 'rationalisation campaign', reducing the choice of models to seven and the engine range to four. There were also fewer options.

The two big casualties were the 5.9-litre '360' engine and the top-of-the-line Chrysler sedan (hence the whole range taking over the big Chrysler's 'C' model designation).

Several mechanical alterations were made to meet the ADR 27A legislation which came into force from July 1976. Both the Valiant sedan and wagon had a '245' (4-litre) low-compresssion Hemi six-cylinder engine which ran on standard (low octane) fuel. This replaced the '215' engine.

New features on the Valiant sedan and wagon included 185 SR radial tyres, a front anti-roll bar, dual horns and reclining bucket seats with a centre cushion armrest. The instrument panel featured a constant voltage fuel gauge and parking brake warning light. The network of interior lights, formerly exclusive to the more expensive Chryslers, was extended to the base-line Valiant.

The 'Chrysler Regal' sedan and station wagon received a distinctive grille taking advantage of the same sheet metal changes. In addition to the items fitted to the base-line Valiant, the Regal was equipped with an engine bonnet ornament, front fender repeater lights and a remote control external mirror on the driver's side. The Regal sedan also had various stainless steel body mouldings and a

'Regal' fuel-filler cap. The wagons featured a 'C' pillar stainless steel applique, special tailgate mouldings and a chrome-plated roof-rack.

The Regal models had revamped seats with cloth trim. The sedan had the 4-litre engine with automatic transmission; the wagon had the 5.2-litre '318' V-8 and an automatic transmission.

The prestige model became the Regal SE. Its release marked the phasing out of the 2920 mm (115 inches) wheelbase Chrysler sedan in favour of the regular Valiant's 2810 mm (111 inches) wheelbase across the range.

The Regal SE had the 5.2-litre '318' V-8 plus power steering, air-conditioning, automatic transmission and a higher equipment level than any previous Valiant or Chrysler. Features included overriders on the front and rear bumpers, quartz-halogen high beam headlights, colour-coded wheel covers and coach lines on the body sides. A vinyl roof was standard, as was a lockable fuel-filler cap with SE ornament.

A fake walnut wood-grain finish instrument cluster included a quartz clock, trip odometer and an ignition delay light. Power windows, a roof console (with front map-reading lights) and retractable front and rear seat belts were fitted. The standard seat covering was cloth, and for the first time, leather was offered as an option. If preferred, the Regal SE could be ordered with the Hemi Six engine and without air-conditioning.

The CL range brought seven new exterior colours, each given a typical Chrysler name treatment: Sundance Yellow, Amazon Green, Harvest Gold, Lemon Twist, Alpine White, Impact Orange and Moonstone Metallic. These were added to the eight colours already available.

The Charger was now available in just one model — the 770. By late 1976 two-door cars were very much on the way out in Australia. GM-H had discontinued the Monaro and the future of Falcon's Hardtop was looking shaky. The Charger, which had once accounted for 50 per cent of Valiant sales, now ran to just 8 per cent.

The Charger 770 also received the new front-end panels and was identified by a honeycomb grille. It had cloth seats, a stainless steel moulding around the front windshield, a glove-box vanity mirror, engine compartment light and dual horns.

The standard Charger engine was a high-compression version of the 245 (4-litre) engine. As with all models in the CL range, the Charger was offered with alternative engines and transmissions. These were the six-cylinder 265 (4.3-litre) engine and the 318 V-8 (5.2-litre) engine, now running on standard fuel.

Transmissions were the manual three-speed, manual four-speed (both available only on six-cylinder engines); automatic three-speed (for the 'Sixes') and an automatic three-speed for the V-8 (with a less direct first gear).

The new Valiant CL front-end sheet metal was carried over to the utility variant, which was back to being named 'Valiant' after a stint of wearing 'Dodge' badges. The CL's higher standard of interior fittings and trim was also carried over to the ute. The 4-litre '245' low-compression engine was standard.

The base CL Valiant sedan was priced at $6309, the Charger 770 at $6948. The top-of-the-line automatic Regal SE cost $11 401.

On 21 April 1977 Chrysler announced its first Australian Valiant panel van. This was the last

Inside the Regal.

The CL Charger 770.

addition to the CL range, and as it turned out, the last 'new' Valiant model.

To aid its research, Chrysler took the unusual step of inviting panel van enthusiasts from all over Australia to visit Adelaide to exchange ideas. The resulting panel van design was aimed mainly at commercial use but offered a range of option packages directed at the youth market.

Chrysler was trying to tap the fastest growing section of the market at that time. The demand for panel vans (for commercial and recreational use) had almost doubled between 1971 and 1976, partly because of the lower sales tax applicable on vehicles classified as being 'commercial'. By the time Chrysler had brought out its entry, this section represented 18.5 per cent of the total commercial vehicle market.

The Valiant Panel Van had the 245 (4-litre) Hemi low-compression engine and a three-speed manual column-shift transmission. A range of engines and transmission options was available.

Equipment included electronic ignition, dual headlights, dual-rate rear springs, front anti-roll bar and power-assisted 280 mm (11 inches) disc brakes at the front. Rear access was via a two-piece tailgate, the upper gate being supported by gas-filled struts.

The optional youth-orientated packages were the 'Sports Pack' and 'Drifter Pack', both designed to make up a van which competed with the big-selling Holden Sandman and Ford Surferoo. The Sports Pack included the Charger grille, quartz-halogen high beam headlights and a three-spoke sports steering wheel.

The Drifter Pack (released a few weeks after the Sports Pack) included bold exterior paint and decal treatment. It was available in three colour combinations (Impact Orange, Alpine White and Lemon Twist) and included the features available in the Sports Pack plus extra equipment including the 4.3-litre Hemi 265 engine.

The Drifter came with a four-speed manual transmission, radial-ply tyres, styled wheels and coloured bumper bars. Some unkind souls suggested that the name was a frank reference to the handling.

The Drifter Pack was later offered with the utility.

The base Valiant panel van was priced from $5308, the Sports Pack-equipped van from $5663 and the Drifter from $6307. In spite of all

the consulting and a 'supercool' advertising campaign aimed at 'surfy guys and their surfy chicks', the Panel Van was a major sales disappointment.

For the year of 1977 Chrysler Australia reported a staggering $28 million loss, though it was not the only company facing hard times. That year GM-H suffered its first loss since the introduction of the 48-215 Holden in 1948. It was $8.4 million down.

In April 1978 — more than 18 months after the CL's release — Chrysler made a number of major improvements to the range. These included a full reworking of the suspension of the Valiant and Regal sedans. The improvements were in response to the battle being waged by GM-H, which claimed that its new 'Radial Tuned Suspension' was vastly superior to that of its competitors.

Ford was also developing a suspension package, but Chrysler beat the official Ford announcement by a couple of weeks.

The Chrysler changes were incorporated as a 'Handling Package' to improve handling, roadholding and steering. Engineers managed to give the car a firmer, flatter ride while improving high-speed cornering, directional stability and steering precision.

Other minor changes included the lowering of the steering wheel position.

Essentially the suspension changes involved a redesign of the rear suspension geometry, the addition of positive castor and negative camber to the front wheels, a thicker front anti-roll bar, shock absorbers with increased damping capacity, and larger diameter rear springs fitted with low-friction interleaf liners and isolating clamps and deeper, softer rear bump rubbers.

The initial press reaction was that Chrysler was merely offering a 'Me Too' Package but many writers who drove the revised car came away impressed.

Motor Manual magazine said:

'On the road the Valiant still feels big, but not cumbersome like it used to. The car feels tight, sure-footed and relays a sense of security to the driver.

'The ride is certainly stiffer — something you have to compromise when going for good handling. However, Chrysler hasn't compromised as much in this area as General Motors did with the RTS system.

'Chrysler is progressing at last.'

No one was pretending that the changes put

Chrysler back to the top of the Big Three but the Handling Package was clearly acknowledged as a good effort.

Wheels magazine heralded the modifications this way:

'Chrysler's changes haven't been as fundamental as GM-H's to its Holden but the Tonsley Park engineers argue that they didn't have as much improving to do. After you fling the latest Valiants through some bends, you can't help feeling they might be right.'

Wheels concluded:

'. . . the new Valiant sedans are better cars — better by a degree that every man will be able to recognise.'

Although the steering improvements came courtesy of Chrysler US (and used some imported components), the suspension work was done in Australia. A story going around at the time was that the local Chrysler people were concerned about their car's understeer and approached the parent company. After the Yanks said 'No sweat, we'll fix it', a CL was shipped stateside. The Americans tested it and sent it back untouched, saying it was the best handling big Chrysler they had ever driven!

Announced at the same time as the revised suspension and steering was the 'Electronic Lean Burn System'. This was a brilliant computer-controlled engine management gizmo which Chrysler initially offered on the 5.2-litre '318' V-8 engine. Fuel savings of up to 15 per cent were claimed during the 18 months' testing which preceded its release.

The system comprised an analog spark control computer located in the engine compartment and a new, more efficient carburettor. Devised by Chrysler Corporation in the US (and in use in US models for about a year), 'ELB' was claimed to incorporate technology developed during the Corporation's participation in the US space program.

Various changes were made to the US system for the Valiant. The new technology, when later adopted for the Hemi engine, brought about Valiant's most marked mechanical improvement since the Hemi's introduction.

The third April 1978 announcement from Chrysler concerned a new version of the CL to highlight the suspension and engine changes. Called Chrysler Le Baron, this new luxury derivative was marketed with a host of additional equipment at a price which saved the buyer $619 over a similarly equipped Regal.

The Le Baron was distinguished by metallic silver body paint and a silver vinyl roof. It came with the 265 (4.3-litre) Hemi engine, improved power steering, cast-alloy road wheels, steel-belted radials, tinted laminated windscreen, tinted side and rear glass, console-shift automatic transmission and bumper overriders front and rear.

It also had all the items fitted to the Regal plus the Handling Package and Electronic Lean Burn System.

A limited production run of 400 Le Barons was announced at a price of $8898. They sold very quickly.

The success of the Le Baron encouraged Chrysler to attempt another special — this was a four-on-the-floor V-8 Charger with 'Drifter' stripes. Only 75 were built with a choice of three colours — white, orange and yellow. As well as the 5.2-litre ELB V-8, the special Charger had a push-button radio, bumper bar overriders and 'Boca Raton' cloth upholstery. The price was $7764.

The run of Charger 'Drifters' just about exhausted stocks of Charger panels and the model was farewelled shortly after. It had had a run of seven years and had been one of the great successes of the local motoring industry.

A total of 32 672 CL Valiants was made. During this model's run Chrysler Australia Ltd celebrated its 25th birthday and the 500 000th Australian-made Valiant.

The half-millionth Valiant was presented by the South Australian Premier, Mr Don Dunstan, to the Adelaide Children's Hospital.

The Lean Burn 5.2-litre V-8.

The Drifter panel van.

The car-based panel van is as Australian
as those famous meat pies, kangaroos
and wombat sandwiches. But Chrysler's Drifter
may well be the end of an era . . .

CAR-TYPE vans don't make a lot of sense. They are neither
a bind to drive nor a real beast of burden. They are the
off-spring of our very restricted production "scales of
economy" rather than market demand.

Or at least that was the way they started off. By adding
some sheet metal to a utility, American-origin makers in
Australia could shift some more of their sedan components.

But to the amazement of even those who thought of the
thing in the first place, these hybrids sold. And sold and
sold.

Everywhere else, the box-type forward control va
dominates the commercial field. But not in Australia.

Everywhere else, the recreational buyers want on
box-vans. But that hasn't happened in Australia. At lea
not yet.

The whole thing seemed so much of a phenomenon tha
Chrysler tried to pretend it wasn't happening. But eventu
ally the wailings of its dealers had to be silenced.

When Chrysler America was told about the need for
car-base van, it couldn't understand why anyone woul
want such a vehicle. But finally, the CL van emerged — th

The last of the

test and probably the last starter in the car-base van ~~ime.

It should follow that by being late in the field, Chrysler ~~uld benefit from the mistakes of its two competitors who ~~ve been selling their vans for some time.

In some ways that is just what happened. Since base ~~ns are base vans, the vehicle with the most interest in ~~e CL range is the Drifter. It is a stripes'n'all attempt to ~~tisfy the desires of the youth market.

Apparently one of those desires is to be noticed, for the ~~020 Drifter kit is extrovert stripes, black paint-outs and bright colours. Really bright colours!

Since we had to muscle our way through a bunch of peering vannies to get to the van every time we parked it, that side of it must work. The other bits you get on your Drifter kit are slightly more functional.

Well, at least some of them are. The Charger front grille is strictly for looks, but the QI inserts in high-beam are worthwhile.

You also get a three-spoke sports-style steering wheel, extra instruments, and reclining bucket seats which have nowhere to recline to.

car-base vans?

The Drifter is delineated from its cargo-carrying co
in full headlining in the rear, and a carpeted load a

Our test Drifter — base price off the showroom flo
$6856 — had the option of Chrysler's beefy 5.2-litre V8
$227) and a T-bar auto (add $162).

After a spate of reasonably interesting cars, we ha
admit we weren't particularly looking forward to dri
the Drifter. But the pre-judgment was formed from ex
ence with other vans and Chrysler's effort was a plea
surprise.

Instead of being a joggling tin-can that handled li
dog, the Drifter was in some ways more pleasant to d
than its stablemate, the Valiant sedan.

But that doesn't mean there isn't room for improvem

For one thing, the load tray has been carried just a b
far forward. This means you are scrunched up agains

ing wheel. Well, maybe not exactly scrunched, but
inly a lot closer than is comfortable. A really big
on would find the driving position very cramped.

e extended load tray also makes a joke out of the
ning seats. The only way you can make the backrests
e towards the rear is by moving the seats right forward
eir runners. By that time, the steering wheel is on top
u.

e wheel is on the big side, and both it and the chrome
rd ball auto-shift look like they belong back in the
es.

e actual steering, on the other hand, is very good. It is
risingly direct and accurate, and yet is not too heavy at
ing speeds.

at probably helps its feel is an almost total absence of
rsteer. If you are with it, the Drifter's handling is very

responsive. It can be balanced up nicely and placed very
accurately on line.

But that tail is never far from stepping out of line, and we
feel a bit of hamfistedness could produce some embarrassing attitudes.

We did not try the Drifter with any kind of load in the rear,
but our guess would be that extra weight would accentuate
the oversteer. A slightly heavier front stabiliser bar should
make the handling just that little bit more forgiving.

It is actually pretty important to get the handling right
because, with the 5.2-litre V8 under the bonnet, the Drifter
is a real projectile.

From a standing start, it is a neck-snapper. Most of the
torque is down low, so there is not much point in extending
the engine beyond its "Drive" shift points of about 3800
rpm.

The coming trend?

BEFORE Chrysler released the Drifter, a number of panel-van enthusiasts were invited to Adelaide to talk about what they wanted in vans.

An interesting point that emerged from that poll is that Australians would like to shift to the forward-control box van that is the universal vehicle of their van brothers in the United States.

The only reason it hasn't taken off in Australia is that there is no suitable vehicle. Toyota and Nissan vans don't really suit the fire-breathing image, while the Transit and Bedford devices are starkly conservative.

But sometimes soon, someone is going to crack that piece of the market. And I think Ford will be first, with a dresssed-up Transit.

One drawback of both the Transit and the Bedford has been that they have been stuck with low axle ratios suited to their original puny English engines.

But the word is that both Ford and General Motors-Holden are working on taller rear axles.

Ford's recreational Transit is said to be already in "the pipeline". Just how far it is prepared to go beyond extra chrome and carpet is unknown.

When you look at the design of a Transit, it would not seem to hard to graft on an up-to-date nose cone. If it looked good enough, it would probably give the traditional car-base vans a big shake.

But I guess there will always be some demand for our car-vans. The last time I tested a Falcon van, I was wheeled into the curb and surrounded by four plainclothes detectives.

"We're looking for a Victorian safe-breaking gang, and yours is the sort of van they use," they said as they flung open all the doors on the Falcon.

And I thought an escape machine was something to do with the great outdoors . . .

Jim Sullivan

Performance-wise, the Drifter accelerates from zero to 60 km/h in 4.1 seconds, to 80 in 6.4, to the metric ton in 9.3, and to 110 km/h in 12.3 seconds.

Our best time over the standing 400 metres was 18.5 seconds, and we were always within a couple of tenths of that figure.

Moving from 60 to 100 km/h with the automatic takes up 5.5 seconds of your time, while 80 to 110 km/h is worth 5.2 seconds.

The flow of power would need a little respect in the wet.

The rear axle ratio is a fairly high 2.92 to 1 and a limited slip diff is optional. For some strange reason, you can't buy a limited slip with a four-speed V8, which would seem to be the very combination which would most require it.

Presumably the "Sure Grip" limited-slip just isn't up to the work it might get from a V8 via a four-speed gearbox.

The brakes are the usual power-boosted disc front, drum rear combo but are much better behaved than you might expect. You don't have to stomp on them very hard to produce rapid deceleration, and they seemed happy to go on stopping without exchanging braking effort for hot cooking smells.

Even more important, there are no dramatics from the rear end, either in the form of lock-up or tramp.

The Drifter scores well on ride and noise levels. The spring rates used might let it drag its tail a little if you want to carry anything really heavy, but they certainly make th Chrysler much nicer to drive when all you want is a sed with sleeping space.

Lining the rear compartment kills the echo chamber e fect of an empty van, and full carpeting keeps mechanic growls at bay.

The rear carpet needs better location, because at t moment it just sits loosely on bar metal.

There is some wind noise, but that's probably on noticeable because everything else is pretty quiet.

The rest is a contrast of old and new. Just how far ba the basic Valiant design goes is highlighted by an absen of face-level ventilation in the dashboard — there is just way it can be squeezed in without a major structural hash.

The instrument panel layout is rather haphazard, and the test car happened to be poorly illuminated.

On the other hand, a neat single steering-column sto controls wipers, washers, dip-light dipping and turn in cators. The heater is rather slow to produce hot air. T heater fan is connected to the ignition switch accesso circuit so Drifter owners need to be careful to turn t ignition key to lock when the van is parked in a garag

Probably the logic of this arrangement was that the d mister could be used at the drive-in . . . which sho Chrysler is still a few years behind.

PRICE
Dollars x 1000

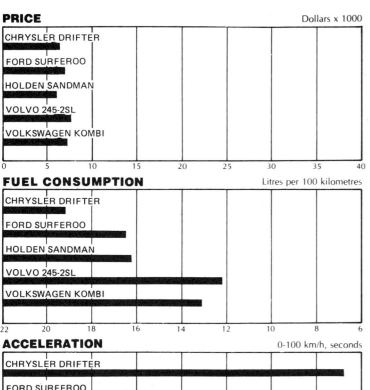

- CHRYSLER DRIFTER
- FORD SURFEROO
- HOLDEN SANDMAN
- VOLVO 245-2SL
- VOLKSWAGEN KOMBI

0   5   10   15   20   25   30   35   40

FUEL CONSUMPTION
Litres per 100 kilometres

- CHRYSLER DRIFTER
- FORD SURFEROO
- HOLDEN SANDMAN
- VOLVO 245-2SL
- VOLKSWAGEN KOMBI

22   20   18   16   14   12   10   8   6

ACCELERATION
0-100 km/h, seconds

- CHRYSLER DRIFTER
- FORD SURFEROO
- HOLDEN SANDMAN
- VOLVO 245-2SL
- VOLKSWAGEN KOMBI

17   16   15   14   13   12   11   10   9

WEIGHT TO POWER
Kilograms per kiloWatt

- CHRYSLER DRIFTER
- FORD SURFEROO
- HOLDEN SANDMAN
- VOLVO 245-2SL
- VOLKSWAGEN KOMBI

21   19   17   15   13   11   9   7   5

THE FIVE-STAR TEST

Comfort	★★
Handling	★★
Brakes	★★★
Performance	★★★★
Quietness	★★★
Luggage capacity	★★★★★

CHECKLIST

Adjustable steering	No
Carpets	Yes
Cigarette lighter	Yes
Clock	No
Day/night mirror	Yes
Hazard flashers	No
Heated rear window	No
Laminated screen	No
Petrol filler lock	No
Radio	No
Tachometer	Yes
Intermittent wipers	No
Rear window wiper	No

CHRYSLER DRIFTER ROAD TEST DATA

ENGINE
Location	Front
Cylinders	8, V-formation
Bore x stroke	99.3 x 84 mm
Capacity	5204cc
Carburation	Two barrel single downdraught
Compression Ratio	8.2:1
Fuel Pump	Mechanical
Valve Gear	OHV
Maximum Power	107 kW at 4000 rpm
Maximum Torque	344 Nm at 2000 rpm

TRANSMISSION
Type	Borg-Warner automatic three-speed
Driving Wheels	Rear

Gearbox ratios
First	2.45
Second	1.45
Third	1.00
Final Drive Ratio	2.92

SUSPENSION
Front	Independent by torsion bar, anti-roll bar
Rear	Leaf springs
Shock Absorbers	Telescopic
Wheels	5.5 x 14
Tyres	185SR x 14

BRAKES
Front	280 mm disc
Rear	255 mm drum

STEERING
Type	Power-assisted recirculating ball and nut
Turns, Lock to Lock	3.5
Turning Circle	11.8 metres

DIMENSIONS AND WEIGHT
Wheelbase	2819 mm
Front Track	1480 mm
Rear Track	1490 mm
Overall Length	4988 mm
Overall Width	1885 mm
Overall Height	1672 mm
Ground Clearance	170 mm
Kerb Weight	1500 kg

CAPACITIES AND EQUIPMENT
Fuel Tank	73 litres
Cooling System	14.8 litres
Engine Sump	4.1 litres
Battery	12V 50Ah
Alternator	40A

CALCULATED DATA
Weight to Power	14.01 kg/kW
Specific Power Output	20.5 kW/litre

FUEL CONSUMPTION
Average for Test	19.93 litres/100 km
Best Recorded	19.10 litres/100 km

ACCELERATION
0-60 km/h	4.1 seconds
0-80 km/h	6.4 seconds
0-100 km/h	9.3 seconds
0-110 km/h	12.3 seconds

OVERTAKING TIMES
50-80 km/h	4.0 seconds
60-100 km/h	5.5 seconds
80-100 km/h	3.4 seconds
80-110 km/h	5.2 seconds

STANDING 400 METRES
Average	18.6 seconds
Best Recorded	18.5 seconds

SPEED IN GEARS
First	75 km/h
Second	122 km/h
Third	171 km/h

CHARGERRR

CM SERIES (1978)

The CM Regal *wagon.*

By 1978 the poor old Valiant was really showing its age. It was no longer possible for Chrysler to cope with the enormous expense of retooling for a completely new car, so the styling department was again given the job of repackaging the 1971 VH design.

The problems with selling a big car in the late 1970s were obvious but an outdated design like the Valiant (which still didn't have flowthrough vents in the dash) was a marketing nightmare.

With the Chrysler Sigma (a Mitsubishi-sourced compact) selling well, Chrysler may have been tempted to drop the big one, but the Valiant was needed to help bolster the company's overall local content. And since its tooling was fully amortised, even a small number could be profitably produced.

On 1 November 1978, the 'new' CM series Valiant went on sale. The big feature was that the Electronic Lean Burn System (ELB) had been adapted to the 'Hemi' six-cylinder engines.

Other changes to the CM were modest. They included higher equipment levels and what the Chrysler sales brochure called 'improved styling features — plus full colour coordination'.

The major benefit of Lean Burn technology was that the hang-on components fitted to the Hemi engine to meet ADR 27A were no longer needed. The new Hemi was close to the pre-pollution-controlled Hemi — easier to start,

more responsive, generally better behaved and much more economical. Chrysler claimed fuel savings of up to 25 per cent.

The CM range was reduced to three models. The major casualty was the excitement machine of 1971 — the Charger. It was dropped along with the poor-selling panel van and utility.

The CM series was identified by the usual facelift treatment comprising a new grille, repackaged tail-lights and varied body mouldings and badges. New nameplates featured the words 'Electronic Lean Burn'. The repackaging was more subtle than with the CL version. This time there was no new sheet metal.

Although CM series vehicles were much better equipped than comparable models in the CL range, there was no comparable price jump.

All sedans and wagons now incorporated the suspension changes introduced with some CL Valiants. Among the features of the base-line Valiant (which Chrysler called the 'medium-line' model) were the 245 (4-litre) high-compression Hemi engine with ELB, quartz-halogen headlights, a push-button radio, 152 mm (6 inches) styled road wheels (replacing the 140 mm/5.5 inchers), a remote-controlled exterior mirror and a heated rear window.

The CM Regal was fitted with the 265 (4.3-litre) Hemi engine with ELB. It also had ignition delay lights, retractor rear seat belts, a trip odometer, a floor console with centre armrest, a Fuel Pacer and bumper overriders.

The 'premium-line' Chrysler Regal SE had 152 mm (6 inches) 'classic style' cast-alloy road wheels and a four-speaker stereo radio/tape-player.

The reduced range included a 'sporty' GLX edition of the base Valiant, which came with the 265 Hemi, four-on-the-floor manual transmission, 178 mm (7 inches) 'Hot Wire' cast-alloy wheels, tachometer, front grille paint treatment, tinted side glass, roof console with map light, rear seat armrest, floor console body stripes and other equipment. The 'sporty' sedan buyer, however, had long since lost interest in Chrysler and the GLX sold poorly.

The prices for the new models were: Valiant from $6850, Regal from $8538 and Regal SE from $12 002.

Chrysler's main advertising thrust now centred on fuel efficiency. In one of its many attempts to win people back to big cars, the company organised various fuel economy tests in which journalists and other independent observers achieved 9.3 L/100 km (30 mpg) and more from the CM in a mixture of city and country driving conditions.

In a scrutineered effort, Sydney adventurer (and long-time Valiant supporter) Phil Gander drove from Sydney to Melbourne on a single tank of petrol.

Most people agreed that the CM was the best Valiant for a long time, but the company had got its act together too late.

In 1979, mainly due to small-car sales, Chrysler Australia Ltd returned to profitability.

When Mitsubishi took over Chrysler's Australian operations in 1980, it continued to crank out Valiants (still with Chrysler badging) but the major sales thrust was directed towards smaller cars like the Sigma and Colt.

By the early 1980s little was heard of Valiant.

In some ways it was an embarrassment to the small-car orientated Mitsubishi. Nevertheless, Valiant was anything but a financial embarrassment. In 1981 it was twentieth on the top-sellers list, achieving about the same sales volume as Volvo. This was a long way from third, but the initial investment and tooling costs were long since written off and Mitsubishi was making a handsome profit on each Valiant sold.

From the buyer's point of view, Valiant was also attractive. The base price in 1981 was $7821 — less than some people were paying for small Japanese cars! Even so, the Valiant's days were numbered.

The CM was the thirteenth model Chrysler had extracted from four basic body shapes since 1962. It was also the last and least successful, selling only 16 005 units in three years.

The last was built in August 1981 (see the chapter 'Requiem').

The basic CM sedan.

Chrysler Regal.

Chrysler Regal really lives up to its name. It's a very special feeling owning a car so luxuriously appointed and tastefully styled.

A classically designed grille, flanked by dual headlights leaves no doubt to the Regal's distinguished pedigree.

A colour co-ordinated interior with reclining bucket seats, richly upholstered in cloth and quality vinyl, cradle you firmly over long journeys. Retractable front and rear seat belts and a rear seat with fold down arm rest give extra touches of comfort and convenience.

Extensive attention to sound-proofing ensures a peaceful journey while you enjoy a little travelling music on your standard push-button radio. A quartz crystal electric clock keeps time accurately, to within a minute every month.

A handy key light guides you to the ignition at night.

A tinted, laminated windscreen cuts down on glare and a heated rear window gives clear vision on frosty mornings. All windows have tinted glass.

Bumpers are protected by over-riders front and rear.

Regal draws its power from Chrysler's 4.3 litre Hemi engine, governed by exclusive computerised Electronic Lean Burn for maximum engine efficiency and economy. A fuel pacer also contributes to economical driving.

From your position behind the padded steering wheel you'll fully appreciate the new instrumentation, reliable Chrysler Radial Tuned Suspension and power-boosted front disc brakes. A 3-speed automatic console shift with high-rise arm rest is standard, or a column shift with

Instrumentation

Front seats with cloth trim

Rear seats with centre arm rest

Valiant Wagon.

Chrysler's Valiant Wagon. It has all the space you've ever needed to carry you and your luggage on holidays and business trips.

Economically priced it's considerably better equipped than comparable wagons.

Push-button radio and clock are standard. So is power tailgate.

Carpeted thoughout the passenger and large cargo area with loop pile, even the doors are protected by scuff pads.

Visibility is excellent and there's a rear air deflector to help keep the rear window free of dust.

Front bucket seats recline at the touch of a lever and there's a comfortable centre cushion arm rest.

A laminated windscreen is standard and all windows are tinted. New instrumentation supplies driver information at a glance. Overriders protect the front bumper. There's a convenient remote control side mirror and inside a prismatic rear view mirror with day/night switch to eliminate glare hazard at night. Quartz Halogen High Beam lights up the road and Convenience lights are fitted in the glove box, ashtray and at floor level. There are two interior lights, one front and one in the back and a handy bonnet light.

Front disc brakes are power boosted and Chrysler's Radial Tuned Suspension keeps you on the straight and narrow. The standard engine is the 4.0 litre, 6 cylinder Hemi engine. Economy is looked after by Chrysler's incredible Electronic Lean Burn ignition system.

The list of options also includes a factory fitted towing package with either the standard 4.0 litre, or the optional 4.3 litre, 6 cylinder engine.

Instrumentation

Front seats with standard trim

Large rear cargo area

Q.H. high beam lights

A whole new deal for when the going gets rough.

It's not every day you or your Chrysler will be expected to handle conditions such as these. Pot holes that try to shake and rattle your bones. Rocks and rubble that attempt to turn your car off the road. Sandy spots and muddy patches encouraging you to make a slip.

Happily, this kind of driving is usually left to the rally driver. The average motorist rarely finds himself facing such extreme conditions. But if he does, he'll truly appreciate the comfort and improved handling and safety factors of Chrysler's Radial Tuned Suspension that rides on sturdy, steel belt tyres.

Chrysler's Radial Tuned Suspension smooths out the pot holes and rough surfaces and makes handling a delight during normal, day to day road use.

On the highway your car will respond obediently and immediately during high speed cornering and sudden lane changes necessary when avoiding trouble.

How we made a good performer, better.

Summing up a good car nowadays is simple. One that performs well, is economical and of course, reliable.

Combining these qualities is not so simple. A car that performs well on the road usually does badly at the petrol pump.

A car that's economical might not be large enough for your family's needs, or have sufficient power to pull your holiday van or boat without feeling the strain.

And reliability? What good is a car that refuses to start on cold mornings or continues to stall in heavy traffic when the heat's on?

That's why Chrysler developed Electronic Lean Burn. A major advance in computerised ignition control and now fitted to all Valiants and Regals. Known simply as ELB it monitors up to six separate engine functions at a time and accurately controls the carburettor and ignition system. A lot of the disadvantages associated with emission control have been eliminated with ELB. So much so, fuel savings of up to 25% have been recorded.* Now that's economy.

While saving on fuel consumption ELB increases overall engine performance. Response to the accelerator is immediate and your engine will start and run smoothly regardless of weather conditions.

*Tested by the procedures stipulated by the Standards Association of Australia for their test no. AS2077/1977.

The ultimate lazy-car

CHRYSLER VALIANT ELB

PROBABLY THE greatest example of the value of Chrysler's Electronic Lean Burn-controlled six-cylinder engines is the company's own V8.

What a waste!

The 5.2-litre ELB-controlled V8 doesn't get the brilliant fuel consumption figures of the six — in fact, paying the fuel bills hurts — yet it doesn't perform as well either.

The latest CM Valiant to excite the electronics in *Modern Motor's* Computester fifth wheel, a 5.2 Regal SE, managed to run from 0-100 km/h in 13.1 seconds, almost two seconds slower than the 4.0-litre six tested in the January issue.

It covered the standing 400 metres in a best of 18.9 seconds, 1.5 seconds slower than the six — its only advantage was a 6 km/h higher top speed.

The Regal SE isn't a hot-shot performer, even by today's strangled standards. It is, however, the ultimate "lazy-car" in the Chrysler line-up.

It's smooth and effortless, from dead stop to top speed, and everything seems to have been designed around that characteristic.

The automatic-transmission shift has lockouts which encourage the jockey to leave it in drive, the oversized feel of the body makes cruising a lot more comfortable than zapping, and the fuel-pacer warning light — located on the front fender, it tells you when you're driving uneconomically — conspires to keep your foot at one-tenth throttle.

The excellent basic handling of Chrysler's "RTS-package" suspension is even well-disguised, by the too-light power steering on the one hand and by the slightly-excessive roll and tyre squeal on the other.

SO THE Regal comes together as an executive's cruiser — as it is meant to be.

And it fulfils the function well, with its plush interior and luxury creature comforts.

The Regal puts its occupants at ease with roomy, good-looking seating covered with armchair-style tucked leather; a clean-sounding radio/stereo; and air-conditioning which does its job extremely well.

Only the hang-on appearance of the air unit interrupts the tidy luxury of the interior.

Power-operated windows, with unusual but effective rocker-type switches, are part of the package. However, there is no driver-controlled lock switch to stop the children playing with the rear units.

The Regal has most of the luxury extras, like carpeting on the lower door trim, retracting seat belts all-round, reading lights, an overhead console with a map light and a power-operated radio antenna.

Instrumentation is average, with four squared-off "windows" in the dash; the two larger ones house the speedometer (with tripmeter) and clock, the smaller ones on either side accommodate the battery

charge/temperature gauges (left) and fuel gauge with warning lights for oil pressure, brakes and parking brake (right).

The four-speaker stereo system, an option on the previous model, is now standard equipment — as are the six-inch alloy wheels.

Other standard equipment items include laminated windscreen, quartz-halogen high-beam headlights, bumper over-riders, and a delay lamp which lights the ignition switch when you get in the car.

It's a luxury cruiser, with all the creature-comforts most people need — if you are after the ultimate lazy-car, grab one . . . it's probably the last of a dying breed.

CHRYSLER VALIANT REGAL 5.2 ELB

ENGINE

Cylinders	8
Bore x Stroke	99.3 x 84.0 mm
Capacity	5205 cc
Carburation	Two-barrel down-draught
Compression Ratio	8.2 to 1
Claimed Power	107 kW at 4000 rpm
Claimed Torque	334 Nm at 2000 rpm

TRANSMISSION

Type	Three-speed automatic
Gearbox Ratios	
First	2.450
Second	1.450
Third	1.000
Final-Drive Ratio	2.920

SUSPENSION

Front	Independent by torsion bars, with anti-roll bar
Rear	Live axle located by leaf springs
Wheels	6J x 14
Tyres	FR78S x 14
Steering	Recirculating ball

BRAKES

Front	279 mm discs
Rear	229 mm drums

DIMENSIONS AND WEIGHT

Wheelbase	2819 mm
Front Track	1495 mm
Rear Track	1502 mm
Overall Length	5017 mm
Overall Width	1894 mm
Overall Height	1407 mm
Ground Clearance	165 mm
Kerb Weight	1652 kg
Fuel Tank Capacity	77 litres

CALCULATED DATA

Weight to Power	15.4 kg/kW
Specific Power Output	20.6 kW/litre

PERFORMANCE

Fuel Consumption	19.6 litres/100 km
Standing 400 Metres	18.9 seconds
0-100 km/h	13.1 seconds
Top Speed	175 km/h
Braking from 100 km/h	44 metres

REQUIEM (1981)

On 28 August 1981 the last Valiant was driven off the Tonsley Park assembly line of Mitsubishi Motors Australia Ltd.

The white automatic CM sedan was Valiant number 565 338. Former chief executive, David Brown, had the honour of sitting behind the wheel. Mr Brown had been managing director of Chrysler Australia Ltd from 1960 to 1972 and, in many ways, was the 'father' of the Australian Valiant.

The last Valiant was presented to Purnell Brothers of Bankstown — a long-time Chrysler dealership which had sold a record 20 000 Valiants. The second last car was the subject of a 'free lottery' among staff at Mitsubishi Motors Australia Limited.

Between 1962 and 1981, total Valiant production included 347 510 sedans, 110 794 wagons, 55 572 utilities, 31 857 Charger coupes, 17 646 hardtops and 1959 panel vans.

More than 300 000 Hemi engines were produced at the Lonsdale plant and Valiants were exported to 35 overseas markets, including the UK, South Africa, New Zealand, Pakistan, the West Indies and, ironically, Japan.

Valiant twice won the long-running *Wheels* 'Car of the Year' award. In 1967 the award went to the VE model. In 1971 it went to the Charger.

Financial constraints had stopped the Chrysler design team from bringing out an all-new model after the 1971 VH. Nevertheless, forward planning continued and many Valiants were designed but never built. The models originally designated VL and CM were to have an all-new body. A second evolution of the CM design, the CM-2, was made ready and work even started on the CN, a major restyling of the planned CM.

None of these reached the production line and the Valiant, once considered a pacesetter, faded away with an image of being years behind its competitors.

Nowadays some Valiants, especially the racing Chargers, are much sought after by collectors and enthusiasts. And wouldn't anyone give their right eye for an original R Series?

THE VALIANT ON THE RACETRACK

The Valiant may have been the most successful Chrysler vehicle used in Australian motor sport but it certainly was not the first.

Chrysler engines and cars have been popular since the 1920s. One of the best known early examples was 'Silverwings', a special based on a six-cylinder Chrysler 70, which was used to break several Australian speed records in 1927. Other Chrysler-based specials competed before and after WW2 and Chrysler production models achieved some success in the REDeX and Ampol trials of the 1950s.

As in the US, the strong, reliable and powerful Chrysler V-8s have been very widely used in drag racing.

In 1970 Chrysler Australia followed the prevailing trend and became involved in motor racing in the hope of boosting sales. The weapon was the VF Valiant Pacer four-door sedan. Although not up with the all-conquering GT Falcon, the Pacer emerged as class winner in 17 races from 20 starts during its first year of competition.

The Pacer was an impressive runner in the 1970 Hardie-Ferodo 500, with the four-barrel carburettor version coming first and second in Class D and the two-barrel model coming second and third in Class C.

In 1971 secret development work by Chrysler (with top racing driver Leo Geoghegan as consultant) resulted in a high-performance version of the Valiant Charger two-door coupe.

Called the R/T Charger, it was powered by a 4.35-litre, six-cylinder engine with three 45DCOE Weber carburettors. This engine developed 205 kW (280 bhp) at 5000 rpm and was known as the 'E38' (see the chapter 'CHARGER'). Surprisingly, the R/T retained a three-speed gearbox. An optional 'Track Pack' included a 155-litre fuel tank, mag wheels and a limited-slip differential.

The E38 made its debut in September 1971 by powering Doug Chivas to victory in the final round of the 'Toby Lee' series at Oran Park. Gloating Chrysler officials looked on and predicted outright victory in the forthcoming Hardie-Ferodo at Bathurst.

Ten Chargers ran in Class D of the 1971

Hardie-Ferodo 500 but were handicapped by heavy tyre wear and fuel consumption. Leo Geoghegan came second in Class D.

For the 1972 Hardie-Ferodo 500, Chrysler released the R/T E49. This had the most powerful Hemi yet, a '265' unit which developed 226 kW (300 bhp), and it was (at last!) coupled to a four-speed manual transmission. Despite its awesome power and speed, the best the R/T E49 could do at Bathurst was to come second and third in Class D.

By 1973 Chargers were uncompetitive, though some continued to race. Chrysler's involvement in motor sport then moved to the rally field, where the Japanese-sourced Galant and Lancer achieved excellent results.

Several Charger specials were used in competition, including Phil Brock's Rallycrosser and John McCormack's sensational Repco 5-litre 'Super Charger'.

Leo Geoghegan in a Pacer 225 (ABOVE) and Charger R/T (BELOW).

"With Philip Brock at the wheel, it's a....

CHARGIN' CHARGER!

Driver going places ...
Phillip Brock

The Chadstone Charger is certainly spectacular, its full-blooded leaps off the Calder mound seeming to head for certain disaster every time.

BRABHAM, Stillwell, Davison, Perkins ... the names are familiar, but they all have something in common. Each has a double-identity to motor racing fans. We all know the successes of Jack (Brabham), Bib (Stillwell), their famous fathers. More often than not, however, success requires no less effort, determination and usually some frustration from these aspirants than any other newcomer to motor sport.

It comes as no surprise, therefore, that the name of Philip Brock has yet to be recognised in the same terms as Peter, his older brother. Until recently, Philip competed in similar machinery, on a similar budget, to most beginners. On June 9, he stepped out of the lower ranks, and is now on the threshold of every driver's dream — a fully-sponsored drive in a competitive car. Enter the Chadstone-Chrysler Charger.

The road to date hasn't been easy, Phil making his first entrance in an FE Holden which he ran once at Calder Rallycross, as well as Bacchus Marsh autocross north-west of Melbourne. At the time, Peter and Philip operated the well-known 'Diamond Valley Speed Shop' in Greensborough, so, while Peter campaigned the HDT supercharged 'Beast' in Division 1, Phil used the Shop's EH panel van in the restricted section at Calder meetings. That the delivery van ever finished a race was in itself a miracle — the Brocks acquired it with over 100,000 miles up as a washing machine service vehicle!

Story and Photos by
MICHAEL JACOBSON

They then proceeded to put another hundred grand on before an ex-cab 179 motor was slotted into the tired frame. After a further 200,000 miles around bush and city, the Van was conscripted at weekends for Rallycross by Phil and Heather Brock (in ladies races) as well! Nonetheless, Division 2 wins in June and September, 1970, showed Phil's potential in such an "anti-race" car, along with several heat wins in his next car, an EH sedan, during '71.

1972 saw the Eastside Chrysler team formed, with Tom Naughton, Jim McKeown

and Philip sharing drives in two 3-speed Chargers. After a promising run in the Calder ATCC Round, a bad smash at Sandown Round 3 in April put an end to Phil's 1972 efforts.

Things began to look up at the start of '73 as Peter Brock vacated his seat in the Holden Dealer Team rallycross car and Phil was selected for the job. Second place in the Division 1 Final was the result in February but an unlucky fourth place in the April Final (Phil finished third, but had copped a 10 second marker penalty) resulted in the HDT unceremoniously dumping him athe night before the June meeting! Later in the year good fortune came in the form of a drive for the NSW Formula One-Europa Charger team at Sandown for Round 2 of the Manufacturer Series, in September. Philip put up a good practice lap (1:21.5) but in the race a broken rocker delayed the car for some 11 laps.

At Bathurst, with Tony Allen driving first up, bad luck again haunted Phil when he took over on lap 43, but pulled out only 1½ laps later with a cooked motor. In November, he returned to the Eastside team, joining Tom Naughton at Phillip Island for the '500K', last round of the '73 Manufacturer Championship. After practising well, Philip started off in a furious dice with Murray Carter's Falcon, dropped back with a pit-stop to free a sticking throttle, but was forced to retire just before half distance when a front wheel bearing welded itself to the hub.

Inside appearance is stark, but neat. Door switches are for wiper/washers, cooling fans and screen demisting unit.

Cooling is no problem, with twin cross-flow radiators backed up by two Thermatic fans, all mounted against the Charger's rear panel.

1974 has seen Phil working as a semi-freelance "wrench", his current project being with the Masseys of Yarraville team on eter anson's new L34 Torana SLR 5000. It was he Chadstone Chrysler firm, however, which ave Philip his big chance as a driver in their ew V8 rallycross Charger.

In its debut, at Calder on June 9, the car von a heat, but missed the Div. 1 Final after itting a marker during another heat. The next neeting at Catalina was more successful, the Charger taking a Semi-final and placing third n the Final, again in Division 1, which at Catalina is based on each particular meeting's eats. Back at Calder in July, the aggregate eat system caused the combination to miss ut on the Final, even though each of the three eats resulted in a win!

There were no problems in September, hough, and Philip cruised to a finals berth by lefeating the all-conquering Renault R8 of 3ob Watson again (he did in July, too) and aking a couple of thirds in the remaining eats. The final was run on a muddy track, as pposed to the dry conditions earlier in the lay, and the Charger was left floundering, lthough it still finished fourth, a little behind fter five laps at Calder. That's some record or a very new combination, and much of the redit goes to Philip's obvious talents as a race lriver, but what of his new mount — the Chadstone Charger?

The car is certainly not so standard, as a irst cursory glance would indicate. However, he body is not lightened, except for perspex vindows, and slightly flared guards belie the rue nature of the machine. Even the grille, umpers and indicators have been left on the ar! Mechanically, however, the car is second o none, and the standard of workmanship is ertainly high throughout.

A 318 Chrysler motor, bored out to 340 c.i., s mounted right alongside the driver's legs, a la Ansett Charger, the front bay being ompletely devoid of engine. This feature is erhaps the largest single contributor to reatly improved traction and handling over ll surfaces. Atop the block is a single 850 cfm lolley carburettor and, although the unit has et to be dynoed, Philip estimates the power to e in the vicinity of 300 BHP, not high by ircuit racing standards. However, the torque igure of well over 300 ft.lb. is of greater elevance in rallycross and stretched from 500 rpm all the way to 5000, giving enormous ractability. Another advantage is that gear hanges are reduced considerably, only 2nd nd 3rd being used whilst in motion.

A Chrysler 4-speed gearbox is used, omplete with Charger plastic knob, but the earwards location of the transmission has esulted in the lever being almost ncomfortably out of reach. The power is then ransmitted through a Detroit Locker LSD to uge 15" diameter steel wheels covered with 1.3" (front) and 12.3" (rear) Goodyear 'all veather' racing tyres. These have proved great n the dry (as at Calder in September), but in et conditions Phil has considered using some ual wheels on the car, which may be used in uture. At Calder he preferred to stick with vhat he knew, but both the Charger and Varwick Henderson's Monaro lost yards to 3ob Watson's agile Renault in the slush. To revent the large rear mudflaps fouling on the vheels, heavy chains are bolted to the nderbody and the flaps' trailing edges.

It comes as a surprise to find the front uspension standard, but the Chrysler has yet o suffer any damage in this area, proving its trength. At the rear, however, a Ford Falcon iT assembly has been substituted, but this is irtually the sole non-Chrysler part of the ehicle. A panhard rod, mounted transversely ehind the diff, helps keep the back wheels ointing straight after jumps, hard cceleration and braking. Three-piston

calipers are utilised on the front discs, with Chrysler drums on the rear. Although brakes are rarely a problem at Rallycross, a booster is fitted to assist retardation.

The cooling system consists of twin cross-flow radiators mounted on the rear panel (tail lights have been replaced by a wire gauze), with a pair of Thermatic electic fans in front. and a pair of large diameter water pipes running trough the left side of the cabin from the engine. Keeping water out of the system still worries some competitors, but the Charger is fitted with the Chrysler electronic ignition system which, according to Philip, has worked faultlessly even through Calder's two water splashes.

The interior has, of course, been stripped of all surplus equipment, leaving the shell bare but functional. Flat metal sheets face the doors, and a shoe-box sized unit on the driver's door houses the ignition key, wiper, washer, heater screen demister and manual Thermatic fan switches. The hefty roll cage of 2" diameter tubing serves a dual purpose, adding a brace between the front and rear sub-frames as well as providing ultra-safe protection for Phil.

From the driver's seat, which is a lightweight shell, for forward view shows a small-diameter leatherbound alloy steering wheel and a flat sheet dash, on which are mounted oil temperature/pressure and water temperature gauges. Sitting atop the vinyl dash cover is a large circular Tachometer, with a tell-tale at around 5000 rpm. Finishing off the interior is a neat, but complex, engine cover which screws over the V8 to leave only a large bulge next to the driver.

In the front bay, a 5-gallon marine-type petrol tank sits low down, surrounded by two 12-volt batteries, wired in parallel, the brake booster, fluid reservoir, heater unit and wiper motor. That's all up front, except for a brace between the fenders for top end rigidity. The wiper/washer system is fed by a 5-gallon plastic gerry can where the passenger seat would normally be, with connections to twin water pumps. One shoots water directly onto the windscreen, while the auxiliary pump sends it through tubes on the driver's side wiper arm.

It goes without saying that the Chadstone-Chrysler Charger is one of the most sophisticated and well thought-out cars on the rallycross scene. All items have been selected for their reliability, duplicated where necessary, and positioned in the car for optimum weight distribution and convenience. Much of the credit for the car's construction and preparation go to Brian Gilbert, Bernie Hopkins and Ray Sherrin, who are justifiably proud of their charge. Proof of their skill as a team has been the car's 100% finishing record to date, with only a few minor problems

cropping up in the car's five-month rallycross career.

The whole Charger project is indeed fortunate to be under ghe guidance of Chadstone Managing Director, Bob Keenahan, who is truly a "live-wire" when it comes to motor sport involvement. Such is his enthusiasm for the team that, should Calder rallycross cease in 1975, the Charger may be converted to Sports Sedan regulations for the coming circuit racing season.

Bob is most happy with Philip's performances, stating "We couldn't ask for more from a driver", realising that the car is still in its early stages of development. Fans will watch with interest the progress of the Chadstone Charger, be it in Rallycross or Sports Sedans, as a welcome addition to the Chrysler ranks. Meanwhile, at 24 years of age, Philip Brock is well on the way to equalling his brother's racetrack record.

'll-natured JOHN McCORMACK charges to the top!

GRAHAM SMITH

Story by DAVID KELLY

AT BURNIE, a small town in North Western Tasmania, some twenty-two years ago a Soap Box Derby was held by the local Apex Club. The Repco Agents entered a billy cart and nominated a young 12 year old to pilot it down a local hill. The youthful driver tore down the slope ahead of all the others to win the event, and it was a proud McCormack family who welcomed John home that day. Little did one suspect that some years later John would renew his mutual relationship with Repco and still be racing.

In the middle of 1973 a group of Motor Race Promotors approached John with a request that he pursue the Sports Sedan category. On evaluation it was considered to be a feasible area of operations and, as Ford and GMH were already strongly entrenched in this area, the decision was made to utilize a Chrysler Charger for this new project.

The design of this new car called for the application of lessons already learnt in the Formula One field. Team Engineer, Harry Aust, was given control of the project and built a vehicle utilising Formula One suspension and brakes and a Repco 5-litre engine beneath a Valiant Charger body, much of which has aluminium panels.

The car was completed and, after tests, had its first competitive outing at Adelaide circuit at the last round of the Tasman Cup meeting in February. Sharing the front row of the grid with Allan Moffat's Mustang, it proceeded to serve notice to the Sports Sedan drivers that here was the vehicle to beat. The Charger beat Moffat's Mustang by a satisfactory margin in its first event that day, but in its next event,

Moffat, by driving his almost to destruction, just managed to grab first place in the last few yards.

Since that meeting, John McCormack's car, now dubbed the Super Charger by race fans, has been a consistent performer and winner on major Australian circuits, including four straight wins — earning $2500 each time — in the rich "Toby Lee" series at Oran Park. In two similar races at Calder, however, John has been struck by mechanical problems when clearly in front, and victory each time has gone to Bob Jane and his Holden Monaro. Nevertheless, John's Charger is a top car, and the modest Tasmanian expects it to stay there for a long time to come.

With his wife and five children, John now lives at Sunbury, Victoria, although his racing activities are still based in Adelaide, where he has established a factory to further develop and build the Repco Leyland F5000 engine. Just as he helped prove the Holden-based F5000 engine built by Repco, so John expects to put the Leyland unit in the winner's circle before too many races have gone by.

1967 Dodge line-up.

FELLOW TRAVELLERS

The body of the 1971 VH Valiant was an all-Australian design.

Earlier Valiants had varying degrees of local design content but were all firmly in the Chrysler family mould. Sometimes the practice was to combine panels from US models with Australian-designed and built sections.

No doubt the following US models will seem at least a little familiar.

1963 Valiant Signet 200 Hardtop.

1963 Dodge Polara.

ABOVE: 1963 Chrysler New Yorker.

BELOW: 1963 Dodge Dart G.T.

ABOVE: 1964 Plymouth Barracuda.   BELOW: 1965 Dodge Dart G.T.

1965 Plymouth Valiant.

1965 Dodge Monaco.

1965 Chrysler New Yorker.

1965 Dodge Coronet 500.

1966 Dodge Dart.
1966 Dodge Coronet 500.

ABOVE: 1967 Valiant Signet. BELOW: 1967 Imperial Crown.

ABOVE: 1967 Valiant Signet.   *BELOW: 1967 Imperial Crown.*

BEYOND THE VALIANT:
THE CHRYSLER-MITSUBISHI CONNECTION

When Mitsubishi Motors Australia Limited (MMAL) took over Chrysler's local operations, it not only acquired a wealth of high quality car-making facilities. It inherited a dynamic team of engineers, designers and managers, many of whom had worked with Chrysler since the first Valiant.

With this team and a wide range of locally built and imported cars, MMAL has managed to succeed in the exceptionally competitive Australian market.

And the locally designed and built Mitsubishi Magna has come closer to challenging the supremacy of the Falcon and Holden family Sixes than any car since... the Valiant.

MMAL was formed as a subsidiary of Mitsubishi Motors Corporation, a Japanese company with a remarkably long history of making cars. In 1917 a founding company had built a Fiat-based car called the Model A, said to be Japan's first production vehicle. Production ceased in 1921, after 30 cars had

been built, and the company did not return to making vehicles until it built Japan's first diesel truck in 1934.

In 1959 the company became serious about passenger car manufacturing. The first modern Mitsubishi was a two-cylinder, 500 mL mini. The Colt appeared in 1962, initially with a three-cylinder, two-stroke engine. A conventional four-cylinder unit was later fitted and small numbers came to Australia.

In 1966 the firm attempted to launch the big six-cylinder Debonair sedan in Australia. It had air-conditioning, automatic transmission, electric seat adjustment and a self-seeking radio. It came at a time when Australians only bought Japanese cars for their low price, fuel economy and reliability. A luxury car was not taken seriously, but small-scale importation of Colt models kept the Mitsubishi name alive.

In 1971 the US Chrysler Corporation bought a 15 per cent equity in Mitsubishi (Japan). Like most US car companies, Chrysler was looking

ABOVE: 1974 Valiant GC Galant.   PREVIOUS PAGE: 1969 Mitsubishi Colt 3-door.

for a foothold in the country shaping up as Detroit's biggest competitor

In August 1971 Chrysler Australia announced an agreement whereby it would assemble Japanese-made Colt Galants and sell them with Chrysler badges. The first, the GA 'Valiant' Galant, went on sale in 1.3-litre and 1.5-litre versions. In 1972 the GB introduced 1.4-litre and 1.6-litre engines and in 1974 the GC facelift appeared. A fully imported GC two-door 'Hardtop' was added to the line-up soon after.

By the time the GD series was released in 1976, 52 000 Valiant Galants had been sold. Local content was being gradually increased and by 1976 it stood at 60 per cent.

Chrysler started to sell Mitsubishi's Lancer from 1974. The small, fully imported car was powered by a 1.4-litre overhead cam engine and was available in two-door or four-door variants. A hatchback with a 1.6-litre engine was introduced in 1977.

The highly successful October 1977 launch of the Mitsubishi-designed GE Sigma sedan enabled Chrysler to take the four-cylinder market by storm. The Sigma became the best-selling four-cylinder car in Australia only seven months after its introduction.

The Sigma was released with three levels of trim: the 'Galant', GL and SE. The Astron 'Silent Shaft' engine was standard in the 1.85-litre GL model and the 2-litre SE.

A GE Wagon was released in September 1978 and a two-door sports version, the fully imported Scorpion, was added to the range.

In the days before the release of the GE Sigma the Australian-based Japanese car companies were trying to find a common 2-litre engine. With this in mind, Chrysler Australia engineers built and tested a four-cylinder version of the Hemi engine. This engine was said to have excellent torque qualities, but as things turned out, it was not used by Chrysler or any other manufacturers. The attempt to find a common engine came to naught.

By 1979 Chrysler had built 50 000 Sigmas and the model was taking 26.7 per cent of its market segment. It did better in 1980 and peaked with 32 per cent in 1981.

1979 saw the release of a locally made 2.6-litre Astron engine. In that year, Mitsubishi Motors Corporation and Mitsubishi Corporation (an associated trading firm) paid $27 million to acquire a one-sixth equity interest each in Chrysler Australia. In April 1980 the two companies paid a further $52 million to purchase the remaining US Chrysler Corporation shares in the Australian company. The name was changed to Mitsubishi Motors Australia Limited on 1 October 1980. At the same time the firm outlined plans to spend a further $150 million on extensions and new equipment.

The GH Sigma, released April 1980, was the last to wear a Chrysler badge. The 1982 GJ Sigma had a completely new body which maintained the same shape and general appearance as the previous model.

The Mitsubishi Sigma Turbo, Australia's first turbocharged production sedan, had been released in late 1981. This model failed to capture the public imagination and a plan to sell a GJ version was dropped. 510 Sigma Turbos were built. In the same year the last Valiant was built and the Chrysler name disappeared from the Australian market.

By 1983 Sigma had lost market leadership in the four-cylinder class but was still selling reasonably well, especially to fleet buyers. The Sigma wagon remained Australia's top-selling wagon.

The 250 000th Australian-built Sigma, a GK, rolled off the Tonsley Park production line in 1984.

The front-drive four-door Colt hatchback, launched in Japan in 1978, came to Australia in late 1980, initially imported then locally produced. Fitted with a 1.4-litre engine coupled to an unusual dual-range transmission, the Colt was well received but sold only moderately well.

In 1982 the RB (locally made) Colt was introduced and a 1.6-litre version introduced. The facelifted RC was released in 1984 and continued to be built in small numbers during 1985 and 1986.

Meanwhile Mitsubishi continued to import coupes, commercial vehicles, forward-control vans and four-wheel drives from Japan. These did well but overall 1982, 1983 and 1984 were not good years for MMAL. The future of the company was resting more and more on the success of a $60 million 'secret' project.

In early 1985 the result of this project — the four-cylinder front-wheel drive Magna sedan — went into production and rocked the industry.

Longer and wider than the Sigma, the completely new sedan was an immediate success and became the first four-cylinder car to compete successfully against the established Australian 'Sixes'.

The Magna was developed from the Japanese 'Galant Sigma', widened and fitted

Chrysler Sigma.

with the Australian-developed Astron 2.6-litre engine mounted east-west. It was offered in GLX, SE and luxury 'Elite' form, and although sold alongside the Sigma, it became MMAL's main thrust into the market.

Sales were so strong through 1985 that the company could not keep up with demand. Adding to the already excellent sales, *Wheels* and *Modern Motor* magazines declared Magna the winner of their annual 'Car of the Year' awards for 1985.

In 1986 the Tonsley Park factory was enlarged to boost Magna production. By late 1986 over 50 000 Magnas had been sold.

Meanwhile, Mitsubishi Japan continued as a major producer of a wide range of four-cylinder cars, as well as light commercial vehicles, trucks and 4WD vehicles. As of 1986 it was the world's tenth largest vehicle producer with 24 000 employees and nearly 200 different vehicle types. Annual production exceeded one million cars and trucks.

As of 1986 the Chrysler Corporation too was looking extremely healthy (thanks largely to the work of Lee Iacocca), producing more than 135 000 cars a month in North America.

Mitsubishi's rebodied 1982 GJ Sigma.

ABOVE: The locally-made RB Colt.
BELOW: The Magna GLX and (BOTTOM) Magna Elite.

POSTSCRIPT: In 1983 — two years after the last Valiant was made — racing driver Leo Geoghegan returned to South Australia's Mallala racing circuit with an R/T E49 Charger. After a few blistering demonstration laps on the 2.6 km circuit, it was clear that time had dimmed neither the skill of the driver nor the phenomenal speed of the car.

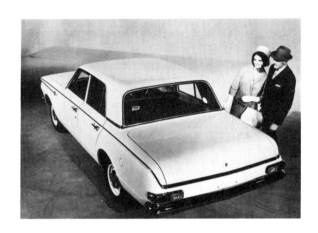

INDEX